AMERICAN
HERITAGE

April 1966 · Volume XVII, Number 3

The place: California, the campus of Stanford University. The time: April 18, 1906. There stood the two great naturalists in marble, flanking an arch of the zoology building. Then the famous San Francisco earthquake let loose. Alexander von Humboldt hung on to his lofty perch, but Louis Agassiz let go and plunged headfirst into the cement pavement. The effect was so startling that a scholar who was passing by uttered a line that will never be forgotten: "Agassiz was great in the abstract but not in the concrete."

AMERICAN HERITAGE

The Magazine of History

AMERICAN HERITAGE is published every two months by American Heritage Publishing Co., Inc., 551 Fifth Avenue, New York, N.Y. 10017. Correspondence about subscriptions should be addressed to: American Heritage Subscription Office, 383 West Center Street, Marion, Ohio 43301. Single Copies: $3.95. Annual Subscriptions: $15.00 in U.S. & Canada; $16.00 elsewhere.

An annual Index of AMERICAN HERITAGE is published every February, priced at $1.00. A Cumulative Index of Volumes VI–XV is available at $5.00.

AMERICAN HERITAGE will consider but assumes no responsibility for unsolicited material. Title registered U.S. Patent Office. Second class postage paid at New York, N.Y., and at additional mailing offices.

Sponsored by

American Association for State & Local History · Society of American Historians

CONTENTS *April, 1966 · Volume XVII, Number 3*

COVER: These two pretty Tory sisters are the Misses Mary (in blue) and Elizabeth Royall, of Medford, Massachusetts, daughters of a colonial grandee, Isaac Royall. They were superbly painted about 1758 by a man just turned twenty years old, John Singleton Copley. He was the first major artist in America, and it is astounding to reflect that as a youth he was painting pictures better than any he had ever seen. Copley has been honored this last year by a large exhibition moving from Washington to New York to Boston, homage from a land he forsook just before the American Revolution. Copley went on to great fame in England, but the fate of the Royalls was harder. Elizabeth died in flight by sea, Mary barely survived the war, and the fine picture from happy days was confiscated. It now belongs to the Museum of Fine Arts in Boston. *Back Cover:* John Gadsby Chapman (1808–89) painted these two humorous self-portraits on wooden palettes; they are in the Valentine Museum at Richmond, Virginia.

THE COMMODORE LEFT TWO SONS

William Henry Vanderbilt   *Cornelius J. Vanderbilt*

—and America's greatest fortune up to that time, some

$100,000,000. The legal battle that followed, full

of tarts and torts and turnabouts, might have been plotted by Dickens

When Commodore Cornelius Vanderbilt expired in New York City on January 4, 1877, with members of his family gathered about his bed singing "Come Ye Sinners, Poor and Needy," he was by far the richest man who had ever died in the United States of America. He had gone to bed for the last time early in May of the previous year. After nearly eighty-three years of strenuous living, his staunch body was finally exhausted by a multitude of ailments, any one of which might have killed an ordinary person. The doughty old Commodore has had his less fervent admirers both before and since his demise, but no one has ever accused him of having been an ordinary person. He fought on through the summer and fall, stubborn and irascible and profanely contemptuous of those whose great expectations were being so maddeningly prolonged by his reluctance to become a decedent.

His residence at 10 Washington Place, then a quiet backwater between the gilded flow of fashion northward from Washington Square and the swirl of commerce up Broadway, was shabby by comparison with the great mansions soon to be built by his favored heirs, and it swarmed with relatives and friends speaking in appropriately hushed voices all through the months of his illness. It must have resembled one of those scenes so relished by writers of popular Victorian novels, with only the favorites permitted to hover solicitously about the deathbed. The aging daughters, who had disapproved of the young wife of their father's declining years

Left: Cornelius Vanderbilt, 1794–1877, called "Commodore" because of his ferries and steamboats, put together the huge New York Central system when past middle age. This portrait of the sturdy old magnate is by Eastman Johnson. Above right: The Personal Column from the Herald *of November 9, 1877—a glimpse at a side of life that rarely gets into history books—contains an ad, signed "Gratitude," which clearly refers to Cornelius J. Vanderbilt (20 letters). One of several mentioned ominously by his lawyers during the trial, it typifies the skullduggery which surrounded the case. No one can say today who "Gratitude" was.*

PERSONAL.

ANGEL—ALL RIGHT, DARLING; TIME AND place you mention. JAN. 8.

DODIE—POPPY HAS SETTLED EVERYTHING; come before 12 o'clock 9th. and you need fear nothing. MAGGIE.

HOTEL BRUNSWICK, WEDNESDAY EVENING; later at another place; will the agreeable parties please address, stating some circumstance? Mr. NORWOOD, Herald Uptown office.

IF THE DETECTIVE, OR FRIEND ACCOMPANYING him, who, in the autumn of 1874, traced a certain gentleman with twenty letters in his name to various dens of vice, will arrange an interview, he, or, should both kindly comply, they, will thereupon each receive $500, or more, according to the correctness of the report. Mr. Webster, see letter, Post office. Address GRATITUDE, box 160 Herald office.

INFORMATION WANTED OF ALBERT SMITH, colored, sister of John, Ellen and Pantha Smith. Address PANTHA SMITH, box 152 Yonkers, N. Y., care of Mr. W. H. Baldwin.

SERVICES OF RELIABLE PRIVATE DETECTIVE can be secured by addressing B. K., station D.

THEATRE, WEDNESDAY NIGHT.—WILL YOU grant the pleasure of your acquaintance to the one to whom you showed your watch, who said, "Ah, 10 o'clock; thank you?" Address ADMIRER, Herald office.

TEXAS.—MAUVAIS GARCON, THE PARCEL IS AT Frenchy's. Telegraph to John.

WEDNESDAY AFTERNOON, SIXTH AVENUE CARS, City Hall to Macy's, then to 40th. Will charming brunette Address CORAL, Herald Uptown office?

WILL GENTLEMAN, WHO FOUND PICTURE AND frame in Madison avenue stage on Wednesday night, return them to Delamater's Iron Works, foot West 13th st.

WILL L. L. MEET ME SATURDAY EVENING, 7 o'clock, corner 7th av. and 23d st. Answer my address.

4TH AVENUE CAR YESTERDAY—BOWED GETTING off 17th st. Address, stating incident, VERNON, Herald Uptown office.

By FRANK CLARK

and whose mere presence now provoked him into violent rages, were relegated to the hallway outside his chamber, from which they could peek in at him reproachfully whenever the door was opened. At an even farther remove from parental favor, downstairs on the parlor floor, a truly classic example of the wastrel and debt-ridden younger son paced fitfully to and fro, still hopeful of winning a last-minute reprieve.

Down on Wall Street the Commodore's old playmates in the game of swallowing railroads waited ravenously. Their mouths already watered in anticipation of the luscious pickings which would be theirs when the old man's controlling interest in the New York Central was divided among a dozen mutually antagonistic heirs. For some of them the strain was too much; premature announcements of his death were frequently circulated in an effort to drive down the price of Central stock, but the great railroad empire that the Commodore had wrested from the wolves of the Street was impervious to such petty chicanery.

Beyond these financially expectant inner circles was the general public, motivated by nothing more tangible than curiosity as to how the richest man in America, having died, would leave his fortune. This curiosity was considerably whetted by the newspapers, which used relays of reporters to maintain a twenty-four-hour vigil about the house and which printed daily bulletins spiced with assorted rumors and conjectures. Even allowing for this journalistic incitement, the extent of general interest in the imminent demise of a private citizen from natural causes seems hardly credible today. But wealth on such a vast scale as Cornelius Vanderbilt's seemed less credible then. William B. Astor, the son of John Jacob Astor, had died two years earlier leaving forty million dollars, but the Astor fortune had been the product of two lives spanning nearly a century, and it was not nearly so impressive as Vanderbilt's one hundred-odd millions, which he alone had accumulated—and mostly in the last fifteen years of his life. Most of the rich men of the time were worth only a few hundred thousand dollars, but in the extremely solid dollars current in those days, one hundred thousand was a tidy fortune. For a man born poor to amass such a fortune as the Commodore's was a phenomenon so baffling to the imagination that even the rumors grossly underestimated its extent.

The funeral took place on Sunday, January 7. It was described as unostentatious but impressively solemn. After a brief service at the Church of the Strangers around the corner on Mercer Street, the cortege proceeded down Broadway to the Battery, crossed by ferry to Staten Island, and there in the old Moravian burying ground at New Dorp, among generations of

The Commodore got the plain funeral he wanted. Here are the

humble ancestors, Cornelius Vanderbilt was laid to rest.

The next day, promptly at noon, the bereaved family gathered in the home of William K. Thorn, a son-in-law of sufficient independent wealth to be on reasonably good terms with all factions, to hear Judge Charles A. Rapallo read decedent's last will and testament. In the macabre gloom customary in the parlors of that era, with the austere and venerable Judge Rapallo presiding, it must indeed have been a grimly momentous occasion in the lives of the two sons and eight daughters who had grown old awaiting it. Phoebe Jane, the eldest, who was sixty-two, barely survived it.

"I Cornelius Vanderbilt, of the City of New York, do make and publish my last will and testament as follows . . ." Thus commenced the document which would dispose of all the vast accumulation of worldly goods of which decedent had died possessed. First, he gave to his beloved wife, Frank A. Vanderbilt, the sum of $500,000 in five per cent bonds of the United States of America, with the stipulation that this bequest was in fulfillment of an antenuptial contract in which Mrs. Vanderbilt had agreed to waive her dower rights. He also gave to said wife the house and lot at 10 Washington Place, complete with stables and all

carriages outside his house in Washington Place January 7, 1877.

appurtenances thereto, two carriages, and one pair of carriage horses.

The second clause, consisting of one brief paragraph, rapidly disposed of five of his eight daughters by giving to each of them outright $250,000 in bonds of the Lake Shore and Michigan Southern Railroad Company. These were nice bonds to own, even without the picture of the Commodore which adorned them, but there may have been outbursts of filial indignation from the recipients, two of whom were already widows, when they and those husbands who were still living realized that this was all they were going to get.

The third clause took care of the three remaining daughters, and though they fared somewhat better than their sisters, they could well have been even more indignant. Their bequests of $300,000, $400,000, and $500,000, respectively, in five per cent government bonds, were securely tied up in trusts from which they were to receive only the income during their lives. Should they die without surviving issue, the principal would revert to the estate and thence to the residuary legatee "hereinafter named." Not a penny would re-

main to console a surviving husband in his old age.

With the expectations of the daughters and their husbands written off so neatly, the Commodore, without even deigning to start a new clause, proceeded to the seemingly more delicate and complex problem of deflating the hopes nourished for a lifetime by his younger son. Cornelius Jeremiah Vanderbilt, then in his late forties, had long been in disfavor with his father. The primary reason was not, perhaps, that he was a frequenter of the plush gambling houses and elegant brothels which flourished in that era of extreme feminine prudery, but probably because he had not inherited his parent's zeal for making and holding money. Ever since young Cornelius could remember, he had been afflicted by a sense of the futility of financial enterprise. The insignificant positions he could obtain and the paltry sums he could earn by his own merits should, he felt, have been as embarrassing to his father as to himself. During the Commodore's lifetime he had avoided such embarrassment by struggling manfully along on an allowance from home so miserably inadequate that he was frequently forced to borrow money from friends, acquaintances, and even strangers. But now, after his life had been irrevocably blighted by his father's money, it seemed only fair that he share abundantly in the source of his misfortunes.

Alas, if the old Commodore had had any sympathy for this viewpoint, it was made apparent in his will only to the extent of preventing his son's life from being further blighted by too much money. After setting up a comparatively modest trust fund of $200,000 in five per cent government bonds, he sternly cautioned his trustees that the income thereof was not to be paid over freely but was to be "applied" by them solely "to the maintenance and support of my son, Cornelius Jeremiah Vanderbilt, during his natural life." Even this miserable pittance was hedged with restrictions. It was only to be doled out if Cornelius' behavior was exemplary. Furthermore, any attempt on the son's part to anticipate, assign, or otherwise encumber this income would result in its being withdrawn from his use entirely. It would "thenceforth, during the residue of his natural life, belong to my residuary legatee." But the crowning indignity was yet to come. "Upon the decease of my said son, Cornelius J.," the will continued, "I give and bequeath the last mentioned $200,000 of bonds to my residuary legatee."

The residuary legatee, as everyone could guess by now, was none other than Cornelius' elder brother, William Henry. This industrious plodder, who scrupulously avoided the haunts of gentlemen, had impressed his father with his reverence for money and his real talent for holding on to it. Cornelius detested him. But he was to be one of the trustees to whom Cornelius would be accountable for his behavior, and this was utterly intolerable.

Next were several clauses devoted to minor bequests to twenty-two assorted relatives and friends of sums ranging from $4,000 to $50,000, and totalling less than $300,000. Then came the grand climax in the eighth clause, which in its entirety reads as follows:

All the rest, residue, and remainder of the property and estate, real and personal, of every description, and wheresoever situated, of which I may be seized or possessed, and to which I may be entitled at the time of my decease, I give, devise, and bequeath unto my son, William H. Vanderbilt, his heirs, executors, administrators and assigns, to his and their own use forever.

Perhaps the full majesty of these redundant legal phrases cannot be properly appreciated without the knowledge that the "residue and remainder" to which they refer was still a little more than one hundred million dollars. The will was dated January 9, 1875, and it was signed, with an awesome abbreviation of testator's Christian name, "C. Van Derbilt," a variation of the old Dutch spelling that he favored.

In a codicil made six months after the original will was written, the Commodore took some $11,000,000 worth of New York Central stock away from his residuary legatee, but that step brought no comfort to his eight daughters and his wayward son. If anything, it was the touch needed to complete their humiliation, for this quite significant little bundle of stock was divided among four of the testator's sixteen grandsons. Five million went to his namesake and favorite, Cornelius Vanderbilt II, and two million to each of the other three. All were sons of the residuary legatee, William Henry Vanderbilt.

We do not know what went on in Mr. Thorn's parlor when Judge Rapallo finished reading the will, but it is not unreasonable to suppose that there were bitter outbursts from the "girls" and that Cornelius must have stalked ominously from the premises leaving a trail of threats about seeing his lawyer. All we know for certain is that William, in his capacity as one of the executors, gathered the precious document to his bosom and departed at once for the surrogate's office on Chambers Street to set in motion probate proceedings that would make him the richest man in America. In any event, rumors that the will would be contested spread quickly.

Disputes over the distribution of a decedent's worldly goods have never been uncommon. They were particularly evident in the United States during the late nineteenth century, when there was a bumper crop of parvenu testators, and the records of surrogates' courts of the period are filled with will contests of sensational bitterness. Like other successful men of

CONTINUED ON PAGE 81
ILLUSTRATIONS CONTINUED ON FOLLOWING FOUR PAGES

The William Henry Vanderbilt family was still one of relatively moderate means while the Commodore lived and when this portrait was painted in 1873 by Seymour Joseph Guy, an English emigrant of limited talent. The pictures on the wall are of no consequence, the fixtures merely serviceable, and two servants are included in the background, perhaps out of affection, perhaps (since they are blurred) for ostentation. The family of any mill owner or banker or local nabob in any small eastern city might have looked the same in those years. From the left they are: father William H.; son Frederick; Mrs. William H.; son George; daughter Florence (later Mrs. Twombly); son William K.; daughters Eliza (later Mrs. Webb) and Margaret; Margaret's husband, Elliott Fitch Shepard; daughter Emily (Mrs. Sloane); Cornelius II's wife, Alice Gwynne; Emily's husband, William Sloane; son Cornelius II. An interesting age: Mr. Shepard was a strict sabbatarian who bought the Fifth Avenue horse-drawn bus line in order to stop its profane Sunday service.

THE INHERITORS
A glimpse at the House of Vanderbilt

THIRD GENERATION

Here are all eight of William Henry's children — grandchildren of the Commodore — plus two of their more notable spouses. These were the château builders, horsy, showy, viewed askance by the old aristocracy until the Mrs. Astor finally left her card at their front door.

Cornelius II, the eldest son, managed the family railroad empire, built The Breakers.

Margaret L. Shepard, a quiet type, built a Y.W.C.A. home and financed Spence School.

William K. and his determined wife Alva (later Mrs. O.H.P. Belmont and a militant suffragette) got the family into Society in 1883 by giving New York a dazzling fancy dress ball, built Marble House at Newport, bought their daughter a duke.

FOURTH GENERATION

Here in battle dress is a group of William Henry's grandchildren, plus two granddaughters-in-law. Of those shown here, the survivor is Harold, who fought Robert Young for the family railroad.

Cornelius III designed a practical new locomotive tender, made brigadier general in World War I. His wife, whom he married over family opposition, was Grace Wilson, who became the great party-giving Mrs. Vanderbilt of her era. He rarely appeared.

Gertrude (Mrs. Harry Payne Whitney), a sculptress of talent, founded the Whitney Museum.

Alfred Gwynne owned a polo field, four yachts, loved coaching, died bravely on the *Lusitania*.

Reginald, a sporty type always at horse shows, married Gloria Morgan, sired the well-known Gloria shown below.

FIFTH GENERATION

It is impossible to find any common denominator but Vanderbilt blood in our sample of the current generation, now mostly middle-aged. Not horses. Not even money. Rebels have appeared, belatedly. There are some public-spirited men, and some genuinely talented ones — but no one rivals the founder.

Cornelius IV, the family iconoclast, was once asked by J. P. Morgan what he would like to become. "A journalist," said the boy. "That's awful," replied Morgan. "Neil" did. It was.

Gloria, in and out of the tabloids for her marriages (notably to Leopold Stokowski), also dabbles in the arts.

Second Alfred G. is an outstanding horseman, like a true Vanderbilt. He owns Native Dancer.

George, once a PT boat skipper like his brother Alfred, has sponsored auto races, hunted big game.

William A. M. Burden, a grandson of Mrs. Twombly, has held many government posts, including that of ambassador to Belgium, is a financier and art patron.

Dave Hennen Morris, Jr., served in two world wars, is a banker. His father, like Burden, was ambassador to Belgium.

Grace, daughter of Cornelius III, married one Henry Gassaway Davis III. After divorce, Davis married her second cousin, Consuelo, at right.

Consuelo, this one the daughter of William K., Jr., was first married to broker Earl E. T. Smith, envoy to Cuba in 1957-1959, a Kennedy crony.

Flora Whitney (Mrs. G. Macculloch Miller) is president of the museum her mother founded.

The Vanderbilts, the ones who have made the headlines now for nearly a century, are all descendants of the redoubtable Commodore's eldest son, the able William Henry. He inherited most of the money, built up the railroad system even further, and launched the family on its highly individualistic course. (See him at left, driving his fine trotters, soberly garbed, the Piccadilly whiskers flying.) Of his numerous posterity, we illustrate a sampling below. Unlike later arrivals in the big money, they are not known for enormous tax-exempt foundations or pious monuments; they did some things of that kind, but mainly they lived interesting, sometimes spectacular lives, as any good aristocracy should.

Emily, widow of a member of the W. & J. Sloane family, later married diplomat Henry White.

Fred, first Vanderbilt college graduate (Yale, '78S) ran a paltry ten million legacy up to over seventy. Education pays.

Florence, as Mrs. Hamilton McK. Twombly, became a lavish, legendary dowager who sent private train for guests.

Eliza married a physician, William Seward Webb, who gave up practice for finance, became head of the Wagner Palace Car Co. He was a famous horse breeder, with a great hackney stable at Shelburne, Vt., owned a vast game preserve in the Adirondacks.

George Washington put up the family's first great baronial palace, the huge Biltmore estate.

Gladys, a retiring sort, married Count László Széchenyi, who became Hungarian minister to the U.S. and Britain.

Consuelo tearfully gave in to Mama and married the Duke of Marlborough, later told her story in *The Glitter and the Gold.*

William K., Jr., encouraged auto racing in early days, then turned to ocean yachting, and set up a marine museum.

Harold, a very active Vanderbilt, invented contract bridge, as a yachtsman has thrice defended America's Cup.

J. Watson Webb, one of Eliza's three sons, won wide fame as a polo player, married Electra Havemeyer, a dynamic collector of American art and artifacts. They personally organized the notable museum at Shelburne, Vt. (See AMERICAN HERITAGE, Apr., 1955.)

Alice, one of Gladys Széchenyi's five daughters, married a count. Three others also wed noblemen, breaking Vanderbilt records.

William Jay Schieffelin, Jr., grandson of Margaret, is 6th generation to have run Schieffelin & Co. (drugs, wines, spirits), a firm founded in 1781, antedating even the in-laws' railroads.

Cornelius Vanderbilt ("Sonny") Whitney has been active in aviation, Democratic politics, racing, mining, matrimony, movie-making. Not to be confused with his cousin, "Jock" Whitney, who is not a Vanderbilt.

John Spencer-Churchill, tenth Duke of Marlborough, Consuelo's son, Sir Winston's cousin, has Blenheim Palace, more titles and hereditary positions than a centipede has feet.

Frederick Vanderbilt Field, Harvard '27, rebelled against his background to join and aid Communist fronts, was once jailed for the Cause.

John Henry Hammond, descended via Emily, is an NAACP official, jazz expert, recording executive credited with "discovering" Benny Goodman.

Alice Hammond, John's sister, liked Goodman too and married the "King of Swing" in 1942.

William Douglas Burden, of another Burden family than William A. M., is a practicing explorer, author, and naturalist.

William B. Osgood Field, Frederick's brother, is a glaciologist and geographer with the American Geographical Society.

Derick V. Webb, son of late Vanderbilt Webb, was recently elected to Vermont state senate as a Republican in a heavily Democratic district.

The present William H., active in cancer research, Florida real estate, and Planned Parenthood, served in the Navy in two wars and was governor of Rhode Island.

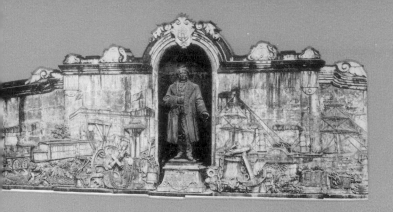

Commodore Vanderbilt lived in a plain house and saw no odds in drinking champagne when "sody water" would bubble just as satisfactorily. His show place was Grand Central Depot (an older one), and one of his few extravagances was the triumphal frieze of trains and steamboats at left, which once stood atop old St. John's Park freight station. (The statue of him alone survives, in front of the present Grand Central.) But how his lucky heirs could spend! America had never seen such pleasure domes, such costly fancies. We offer a glimpse of them here.

FRUITS OF THE LEGACY

Unlike the Fifth Avenue châteaux, most of the Vanderbilt country mansions still stand. This was Margaret Louisa Shepard's place, now the Sleepy Hollow Country Club at Scarborough, N. Y.

Fred built Rough Point (above) in Newport; Mrs. Twombly roughed it (below) in Madison, N. J.

For George Washington Vanderbilt II's stunning Biltmore, at Asheville, N.C., Richard Hunt took ideas from Chambord and Blois in France; F. L. Olmsted did landscaping, Gifford Pinchot the forests.

One also built for the public

Old Vanderbilt Clinic, Sloane Maternity Hospital, College of Physicians and Surgeons were early family benefactions, now moved uptown.

St. Bartholomew's doors, a gift, designed by Stanford White.

Former Vanderbilt Hotel, on Park Ave., will be apartments.

The Commodore founded Vanderbilt University with one million. Descendants have given another 25. Harold heads its board.

Unable to get boxes at earlier hall, Vanderbilts backed a new Metropolitan Opera.

And indulged many mighty whims

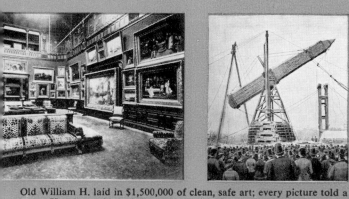

Old William H. laid in $1,500,000 of clean, safe art; every picture told a story. He also paid to bring this obelisk, Egypt's gift, to New York.

The Coronet Sweepstakes, once a main event for the Four Hundred, found the Vanderbilts steady scorers; one duke, four counts, one earl, one plain "hon."

One can, given a fortune big enough, collect anything. For instance, the large tortoise (right) was picked up in the South Seas by William K. Jr., who showed such marine exhibits at his Centerport, L. I., house (row above). Nicholas Murray Butler, on the other hand, was "collected" by George Washington Vanderbilt II when in 1887 he gave "brain money" and later land to a struggling young educational association. The money hired Butler (later president of Columbia, a Nobel Prize winner in 1931), and the result was Teachers College, a force in U.S. education.

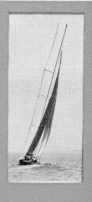

One's house was definitely one's castle

Vanderbilt town houses dominated Fifth Avenue from No. 640 (above, left) at 51st Street all the way up to 58th. William H. built himself 640. His daughters Margaret and Emily occupied the adjoining twin mansion, partly visible. The last of these houses to come down, 640 paid taxes of $184 a night by 1941.

Richard Morris Hunt was the architect of W. K. Vanderbilt's Renaissance château at 660. Just showing at right is the manse of his son W. K., Jr., at No. 666.

684 was Florence Vanderbilt Twombly's; at left once stood sister Eliza Webb's.

Cornelius II carried on his almost excessively blameless life in this block-long castle at 57th Street. He once moved his bedroom to avoid shock of a rear view of a naked stone nymph in a city fountain.

Should Cornelius II weary of his city castle he could go to his Newport "cottage," The Breakers.

Not far from The Breakers, Cornelius II's brother William K. built (as a birthday favor for his wife Alva) Marble House, a kind of seaside White House in white Italian marble, looming enormously on what Henry James called a "miniature spot of earth." It cost two million to build, nine more to decorate.

Thrifty Fred sold off Rough Point but kept a place at Bar Harbor, put up a mansion in Hyde Park for mere $660,000.

Palm Beach is full of Vanderbilts; Harold's house appears above. Finally most Vanderbilts go to the vault (right) on Staten Island.

G. W. II gave city a library.

Electra Webb moved old lighthouse, plus a steamboat, to her dry-land museum at Shelburne.

Vanderbilt Hall, one of several gifts the family gave Yale, was memorial by Cornelius II to his son William H., who died in college. It cost $575,000. Room 31 was reserved for any Vanderbilts matriculating at Yale.

Long Island mansion of W. K. Vanderbilt, Jr., now museum of fish, shells, art, antiques.

Architect Marcel Breuer's model shows soon-to-be-completed Whitney Museum of American Art, third building to house collection begun by sculptress Gertrude Whitney.

With his J boat *Ranger* (left) Harold won 1937 America's Cup. Yachting has been a Vanderbilt specialty ever since the Commodore steamed *en famille* to Europe with his *North Star* in 1853. The ship above is W. K. Jr.'s *Alva*, 264 feet long, which carried a seaplane and cost in all $2,500,000. She was delivered in 1931, when Central stock sank to 25 from the 1929 high of 256½. Trouble? No, the family by then owned relatively little of the railroad.

A Vanderbilt auto racing cup

Blood will tell, especially a railroad man's. According to Wayne Andrews in *The Vanderbilt Legend*, after Gladys wed Count Széchenyi and went to live in Budapest, she soon controlled the local trams. She was decorated for her war relief work there.

Vanderbilts have always loved horses—for trotting, polo, coaching, racing. Alfred's Native Dancer won $513,425 in his best year (1953). Sonny Whitney's stable (above) was huge; Dr. Webb's in Shelburne seemed even bigger. The Commodore loved fast trotters, and son William broke the mile record with his famous trotting horse Maud S. In Paris, senior W. K. thrice won the Prix du Jockey Club.

By JOHN STANDS IN TIMBER

Edited and with an introduction by MARGOT LIBERTY

Last Ghastly Moments
at the Little Bighorn

*A Cheyenne historian whose grandfather was in the battle
sheds new light on the slaughter of Custer and his troopers*

So much has been written about the Battle of the Little Bighorn that it would seem that everything that can be said about it is already known. But interest in the slaughter of some 225 soldiers and civilians under Lieutenant Colonel George Custer by Sioux and Northern Cheyenne warriors in June of 1876 has remained high, and the search for new scraps of information about it continues unabated. At the heart of this interest is a mystery which has never been fully solved. It is this: How was it that Custer and all his men were killed?

Some students of Indian warfare have speculated that the warriors simply wore down the surrounded troopers of Custer's Seventh Cavalry from a distance until casualties were so severe that they could ride in on the survivors. But, in direct contradiction to this, others point to many notable Indian fights of the Plains (Beecher Island, the Wagon Box, the Big Hole, and even another sector of the Little Bighorn battle itself—the attack on Custer's subordinates, Major Marcus Reno and Captain Frederick Benteen) to show that such tactics would have been contrary to Indian

Opposite: The Custer battlefield today, with the site of the Last Stand enclosed by a fence. The stones, which were erected in 1890, mark approximately where Custer's men fell and were originally buried. Almost all of the officers who could be identified were reburied elsewhere in 1877. Custer, whose stone is at left center, was reinterred at West Point. In 1881, the bodies of the enlisted men were moved to a common grave on this ridge. Scattered down the hillside are stones that mark the places where troopers fell who may have been trying to fight their way up to join Custer. The huge Indian encampment stretched out across the plain beyond the trees lining the banks of the Little Bighorn.

custom. In all of these cases the Indians encircled troops for long periods of time, riding around the besieged whites at a safe distance, potshotting at them, dashing at them from time to time, and finally breaking off the engagement and riding away.

Such tactics were traditional with the Plains Indians. Once the warriors were satisfied that they had acquitted themselves well and gained honors, had halted the enemy and rendered him powerless, or had secured their camps and enabled their women and children to get safely away, they saw no sense in risking further the lives of their brave men. This was especially true when the Indians began to suffer casualties; then the chiefs would usually counsel their men to end the fight quickly and withdraw.

The following document suggests a hitherto unsuspected factor in the battle: a group of warriors who formed a kind of suicide squad. Their example may provide an explanation of why Custer's detachment was slaughtered to the last man. Nothing resembling this story has appeared in any previous account of the fight. The question naturally arises, Why not? One answer is that only a comparatively few individuals in the two tribes knew enough about the event to talk about it, and white questioners never happened to talk to these individuals. Another and more likely answer is that those who did know about it considered it too revered a rite to discuss with the race that had conquered them.

It should be remembered that Indians were the only surviving witnesses to the Last Stand and that everything written about Custer's final moments stems from these Indian informants. The value of many of these accounts is questionable. Most were collected, under

15

extreme pressure, soon after the battle. The Indians who did talk feared, on the one hand, punishment by the whites, and on the other, contempt from their own people for being informers. Under these circumstances, they often said what they thought their questioners wanted them to say, and concealed information which they thought might bring trouble upon the Indians. They also withheld information concerning tribal customs and beliefs which they felt they had no right to impart to white men, or which white men might have

About 1898, some twenty-two years after the Custer massacre, the artist Frederic Remington asked Kicking Bear, a veteran of the Little Bighorn, to paint this pictograph of the battle. Custer, in yellow buckskin, is shown dead at left center, while braves ride down the last of his command. The figures in outline at top left are the departing spirits of dead soldiers. In the village at lower right, Sioux women—one with a captured American flag—prepare a victory celebration. The four central standing figures are (left to right): Sitting Bull, Rain in the Face, Crazy Horse, and the artist, Kicking Bear.

misunderstood. Thus it is not surprising that a number of events at the Little Bighorn went unrecorded except in the oral traditions of the tribes who fought there.

The story that follows is based entirely on the traditions of the Northern Cheyennes, who today live in Montana close to the field on which their forebears fought Custer. The battle accounts were gathered with care and devotion over many years by John Stands in Timber, a Northern Cheyenne who some fifty years ago dedicated himself to the task of being the historian of his people. He decided then that when the time was right he would tell the white man the history of his tribe as his own people knew it. Stands in Timber, a grandson of Lame White Man, who was killed at the Little Bighorn, was educated at the Haskell Institute, a school for Indians in Lawrence, Kansas, and part of his dedication to the history of his people is the result of hearing white men's versions of events that contradicted what the Indians knew. After returning to the reservation from Haskell, he began to collect tribal stories, gathering them, when possible, from eyewitnesses to and participants in important events. The fear of punishment by whites and the reluctance to reveal many aspects of Indian history persisted among his people for decades. But the old people of the tribe who might be hurt or who might resent the recording of their actions for the whites are now dead. Today, with John Stands in Timber in his eighties, his document can at last be made public.

It will be helped by a brief summation of what is already known of the battle. The command led by Colonel Custer had been an element in a three-pronged drive designed to trap a large group of Sioux and Northern Cheyennes who had refused to go onto their reservations. One prong, commanded by General George Crook, moving north into Montana from the North Platte River, had been mauled and turned back by Sioux and Northern Cheyennes at the Rosebud River on June 17, 1876. The second prong, troops from western Montana, and the third prong, a force moving west from the Missouri River, had met on the Yellowstone at the mouth of the Rosebud. In the third prong was Custer's Seventh Cavalry. Unaware of Crook's withdrawal, the troops on the Yellowstone now planned to turn south and catch the hostile Indians between themselves and Crook's force.

One unit, under Colonel John Gibbon, was ordered to go up the Yellowstone to the Bighorn, then march south along that river to the Little Bighorn. Custer was directed to move south along the Rosebud, parallel to Gibbon; the idea was to trap the Indians between them. Custer, it is believed, was to make a leisurely march and not start across from the Rosebud to the Little Bighorn until the evening of June 25, when Gibbon would have had time to arrive opposite him for a joint attack on June 26. The units separated, and at noon on June 22, Custer started up the Rosebud with some six hundred soldiers, forty-four Arikara and Crow Indian scouts, about twenty packers and guides, and a civilian newspaper correspondent named Mark Kellogg.

The Sioux and Northern Cheyenne warriors who had repulsed Crook on the Rosebud had meanwhile moved their camps to the Little Bighorn. Their villages, set up in five large circles of tepees and several smaller ones, stretched about three miles along the river's west bank. The northernmost circle was the village of the Northern Cheyennes, while at the south was that of Sitting Bull's Hunkpapa Sioux. Between them were Oglalas and other Sioux, together with a small number of Arapahoes. There were probably some ten thousand Indians present, of whom at least three thousand were fighting men.

Custer came up the Rosebud, but on learning from scouts that the hostiles were west of him on the Little Bighorn, turned in that direction, and on the morning of June 25 was ready to do battle alone, without waiting for Gibbon. After surveying the valley of the Little Bighorn, but failing to see the Indian camp and thus understand its exact size and population, he divided his men into four units. One was left in the rear to protect the slow-moving pack train. A second, under Captain Frederick Benteen, was sent to scout the hills to the southwest and to prevent the escape of the Indians in that direction. The third, under Major Marcus Reno, was ordered to attack the camp at its southern end, while Custer took the remaining unit of about 225 men to strike the northern end and catch the Indians between his troops and Reno's.

The Indian forces, of course, were much bigger than Custer had suspected. Reno's men, accompanied by Arikara scouts, had a sharp battle in the valley, mainly with Sitting Bull's Hunkpapas; after heavy losses, they retreated to a high bluff across the Little Bighorn from the Indian camp, where they were soon joined by the pack train and Benteen. Heavy firing could be heard from Custer's direction and an attempt was made to reach him, but it failed. Reno and Benteen then stood off the Indians all night and the next day. The rest of the troops from the Yellowstone arrived the morning of the twenty-seventh. The Indian camp had disbanded the evening of the twenty-sixth. No further fighting had seemed necessary to the Indians, and they had all moved away, out of range of the troops.

Custer's command was discovered entirely destroyed.

With that background, one can now read John Stands in Timber's account. —*Margot Liberty*

"After the suicide boys came in, it did not take long"

HE attack of Colonel Custer on the Northern Cheyennes and Sioux did not surprise the Indians as much as many people think. They knew the soldiers were in the country looking for them, and they expected trouble, though they did not know just when it would come. My grandfather, Lame White Man, told my grandmother, Twin Woman, the morning before the fight that scouts had reported soldiers on the Rosebud, and when they went farther down [the Rosebud] they also saw the steamship that had brought them supplies, there in the Yellowstone River. White Man Bear's people were on their way to the Black Hills when they saw them. They did not turn back, but kept on their way, but they met other scouts coming this way and gave them the news. It was after that that the word spread.

The Sioux leaders in the villages sent word that they wanted all the chiefs to gather to discuss what to do if the soldiers approached. They had decided not to start anything, but to find out what the soldiers were going to do, and talk to them if they came in peacefully. "It may be something else they want us to do now, other than go back to the reservation," they said. "We will talk to them. But if they want to fight we will let them have it, so everybody be prepared."

They also decided that the camp should be guarded by the military bands, to keep individual warriors from riding out to meet the soldiers. It was a great thing for anyone to do that—to go out and meet the enemy ahead of the rest—and the chiefs did not want this to happen. So it was agreed that both the Sioux and Northern Cheyenne military bands would stand guard. Each band called its men, and toward evening they went on duty. Bunches of them rode to ten or fifteen stations on both sides of the Little Bighorn where they could keep good watch. About sundown, they could be seen all along the hills there.

There was good reason for them to watch well. The people usually obeyed the orders of the military bands. Punishment [ranging from a beating to destruction of horses, tepees, or other property] was too severe if they did not. But that night young men [who had not yet gained war honors, and in their eagerness to achieve them often put personal goals above tribal welfare] were determined to slip through. Soon after the bands had begun patrolling, my stepgrandfather's friend, Bigfoot, came to him. "Wolftooth," he said, "we could get away and go on through. Maybe some others will too, and meet the enemy over on the Rosebud."

They began watching to see what the military bands were doing, and to make plans. They saw a bunch of them start across to the east side of the river and another bunch on the hill between what became the Reno and Custer battlefields. Many more were on the high hills at the mouth of Medicine Tail Creek. So they decided what to do. After sundown they took their horses way up on the west side of the river and hobbled them, pretending to be putting them there so they could get them easily in the morning. Then they returned to camp. But when it was dark, they walked back out there and got the horses, and went back down to the river. When they did, they heard horses crossing and were afraid to go ahead. But the noise died away, and they went on into the river slowly, so even the water would splash more quietly. They got safely to the other side and hid in the brush all night there so they would not be discovered.

In the meantime, there was some excitement in the camp. Some of the Sioux boys had just announced that they were taking the suicide vow, and others were putting on a dance for them at their end of the camp. This meant that they were throwing their lives away. In the next battle they would fight till they were killed. The Northern Cheyennes claimed that they had originated the suicide vow; then the Sioux learned it from them, and they called this dance they put on to announce it "Dying Dancing."

A few Northern Cheyenne boys had announced their decision to take the vow at the same time, so a lot of Northern Cheyennes were up there in the crowd watching. Spotted Elk and Crooked Nose are two that remembered that night and told me about it. They said the people were already gathering, early in the evening. By the time they got to the upper end there, a big place had been cleared and they were already dancing. When those boys came in, they could not hear themselves talk, there was so much noise, with the crowd packed around and both the men and women singing.

They did not remember how many took part, and never thought of counting them, but Spotted Elk said later there were not more than twenty. They remembered the Northern Cheyenne boys that were dancing: Little Whirlwind, Cut Belly, Closed Hand, and Noisy Walking. They were all killed the next day. But none of them knew that night that the soldiers were coming next day for sure; they were just suspicious.

The next morning the Indians held a parade for the boys who had been in the suicide dance the night before. Different ones told me about it; one was my grandmother, Twin Woman, the wife of Lame White Man, the only Northern Cheyenne chief who was killed in the battle. It was customary to put on such a parade after a suicide dance. The boys went in front, with an old man on either side announcing to the public to look at these boys well; they would never come back after the next battle.

They paraded down through the Northern Cheyenne camp on the inside and back on the outside, and then returned to their own village.

While the parade was still going on, three boys went down to the river to swim: William Yellowrobe, Charles Headswift, and Wandering Medicine. They were down there in the water when they heard a lot of noise, and thought the parade had just broken up. Some riders in war clothes came along the bank yelling and shooting. Then somebody hollered at them, "The camp is attacked by soldiers!" So they never thought about swimming any more. They jumped out and ran back to their families' camps. Headswift's people had already run away toward the hills at the west, but his older brother came back after him. They had to run quite a distance to get his brother's horse. Then they rode double to join the women and children where they were watching the beginning of the fight.

Meanwhile, after the parade had ended, my grandmother said a man named Tall Sioux had put up a sweat lodge, and Lame White Man went over to take part in his sweat bath there. It was just a little way from the tepees. She said they had closed the cover down a couple of times—they usually did it four times in all, pouring water over the hot stones to make steam —and the second or third time, the excitement started in the valley above the village [where Reno was attacking the Hunkpapas]. She did not see which way the soldiers came, but there were some above the village. And some more [Custer's troops] came from straight across the river.

The men in the sweat tepee crawled out and ran to help their families get on horses and get away. Lame White Man did not have time to get war clothes on. He just wrapped a blanket around his waist and grabbed his moccasins and belt and a gun. He went with Grandmother a little way to the west of some small hills there. Then he turned down below and crossed after the rest of the warriors.

Of course, Wolftooth and Bigfoot had come out of the brush long before then. At daylight they could see the Indian military patrols still on the hills, so they waited for some time. They moved along, keeping under cover, until they ran into more warriors and then some more. Close to fifty men had succeeded in slipping through the military bands and crossing the river that way. They got together and were about halfway up a wooded hill [about four miles east of where the battle was to occur] when they heard someone hollering. Wolftooth looked back and saw a rider on a ridge a mile below them, calling and signalling them to come back.

They turned and galloped back, and when they drew near, the rider began talking in Sioux. Bigfoot could understand it. The soldiers had already ridden down toward the village. Then this party raced back up the creek again to where they could follow one of the ridges to the top, and when they got up there, they saw the last few soldiers going down out of sight toward the river—Custer's men. Reno's men had attacked the other end already, but they did not know it.

As the soldiers disappeared, Wolftooth's band split up. Some followed the soldiers, and the rest went on around a point to cut them off. They caught up there with some that were still going down, and came around them on both sides. The soldiers started shooting; it was the first skirmish of the Custer part of the battle, and it did not last very long. The Indians said they did not try to go in close. After some shooting, both bunches of Indians retreated back to the hills, and the soldiers crossed the south end of the ridge.

The soldiers followed the ridge down to the present cemetery site. Then this bunch of forty or fifty Indians came after them again and started shooting down at them a second time. But the soldiers were moving on down toward the river, across from the Northern Cheyenne camp. Some of the warriors there had come across, and they began firing at the soldiers from the brush in the river bottom. This made the soldiers turn north, but then they went back in the direction they had come from, and stopped when they got to where the cemetery is now. And they waited there—twenty minutes or more. [It may be noted that this Cheyenne version places Custer's farthest advance a mile or so beyond and west of the ridge where he died and has him retreat to that final position. The most generally accepted story up to now is that he was cut down along the ridge as he moved from the southeast toward the site of his final stand.] The Indians have a joke about his long wait. Beaver Heart said that when the scouts warned Custer about the village, he laughed and said, "When we get to that village, I'm going to find the Sioux girl with the most elk teeth on her dress and take her along with me." So that is what he was doing those twenty minutes. Looking.

Wolftooth and his band of warriors moved in meanwhile along the ridge above the soldiers. Custer went into the center of a big basin below where the monument is now, and the soldiers of the Gray Horse Com-

Custer was fond of unusual uniforms (see page 58); on the plains he wore buckskins, plus a wide-brimmed hat to protect his fair skin against the sun. He was photographed with Indian scouts in Montana in 1873, while he was guarding Northern Pacific construction workers against the hostiles.

pany [Company E, under Lieutenant Algernon Smith] got off their horses and moved up on foot. If there had not been so many Indians on the ridge above, they might have retreated over that way, either then or later when the fighting got bad, and gone to join Reno. But there were too many up above, and the firing was getting heavy from the other side now.

Most of the Northern Cheyennes were down at the Custer end of the fight, but one or two were up at the Reno fight with the Sioux. Beaver Heart saw Reno's men come in close to the Sioux village and make a stand there in some trees after they had crossed the river. But they were almost wiped out. They got on their horses and galloped along the edge of the cottonwood trees on the bank and turned across the river, but it was a bad crossing. The bank on the other side was higher, and the horses had to jump to get on top. Some fell back when it got wet and slick from the first ones coming out, and many soldiers were killed trying to get away. Some finally made it up onto the hill where they took their stand.

It was about that time that Custer was going in at the lower end, toward the Cheyenne camp. It was hard to keep track of everything at the two battles. A number of Indians went back and forth between the two, but none of them saw everything. Most of them went toward the fight with Custer, once Reno was up

on the hill. Wolftooth said they were all shooting at the Custer men from the ridge, but they were careful all the time, taking cover.

Before long, some Sioux criers came along behind the line, and began calling in the Sioux language to get ready and watch for the suicide boys. They said they were getting ready down below to charge together from the river, and when they came in, all the Indians up above should jump up for hand-to-hand fighting. That way the soldiers would not have a chance to shoot, but would be crowded from both sides. The idea was that they had been firing both ways. When the suicide boys came up, they would turn to them and give those behind a chance to come in close. The criers called out those instructions twice. Most of the Cheyennes could not understand them, but the Sioux there told them what had been said.

So the suicide boys were the last Indians to enter the fight. Wolftooth said they were really watching for them, and at last they rode out down below. They galloped up to the level ground near where the museum is now; some turned and stampeded the gray horses of the soldiers. By then they were mostly loose, the ones that had not been shot. The rest of the boys charged right in at the place where the soldiers were making their stand, and the others followed them as soon as they got the horses away.

The suicide boys started the hand-to-hand fighting, and all of them were killed there or were wounded and died later. When the soldiers started shooting at them, the Indians above with Wolftooth came in from the other side. Then there was no time for the soldiers to take aim or anything. The Indians were right behind and among them. Some soldiers started to run along the edge under the top of the ridge, and for a distance they scattered, some going on one side and some the other. But they were all killed before they got far.

At the end it was quite a mess. They could not tell which was this man or that man, they were so mixed up. Horses were running over the soldiers and over each other. The fighting was really close, and they were shooting almost any way without taking aim. Some said it made it less dangerous than fighting at a distance; then the soldiers would aim carefully and be more likely to hit you. After they emptied their pistols this way, there was no time to reload. Neither side did. But most of the Indians had clubs or hatchets, while the soldiers just had guns; they were using those to hit with and knock the enemy down. A Sioux, Stinking Bear, saw one Indian charge a soldier who had his gun by the barrel, and he swung it so hard he knocked the Indian over and fell over himself.

Yellow Nose was in there close. He saw two Indian

CONTINUED ON PAGE 72

21

Champney painted the broad and shady common in Old Deerfield about a year after he moved there with his family in 1876.

THIS IS TRANQUIL DEERFIELD

Traffic is heavy on U.S. 5 running north from Springfield, Massachusetts, up into the vacation lands of Vermont and New Hampshire. Not far from the Vermont border the road signs say "Deerfield"— but most drivers neither stop nor slow down, for the village lies to one side, a quarter of a mile off the highway. They thereby miss one of the most fascinating of New England's communities—rich in historic memories, with many old and wonderful houses and few modern "improvements" to mar the peaceful village atmosphere.

One potent force in keeping Deerfield much the way it was in the eighteenth century, when it was rebuilt after the infamous Deerfield Massacre of 1704, has been Deerfield Academy, a distinguished school that has educated American boys steadily since its founding in 1797. Dr. Frank L. Boyden, Deerfield's famous headmaster, and the trustees have long encouraged preservation of the character of the old village—something they have been able to do effectively because the academy owns and maintains a number of colonial houses which are inhabited by faculty members and other

In a photo of a snowy scene on Deerfield's main street, the bearded Champney stands by a sleigh, looking toward his home.

As It Looked Ninety Years Ago . . .

villagers. The result is that visitors to Deerfield today might easily recognize it from the views seen above.

The boys at Deerfield take a considerable interest in the historic surroundings of their school, though in general their enthusiasm, divided between scholarly matters and such natural concerns as skiing, electric guitars, and girls, is not especially remarkable. About two years ago, however, nine members of the junior class who happened to be unusually interested in the history of American culture put their heads together and decided to make better use of the rare advantages

of Deerfield.* Almost immediately, they found a helpful ally in the Heritage Foundation (no connection with AMERICAN HERITAGE), established at Deerfield in 1952 by Mr. and Mrs. Henry Flynt for the purpose of preserving collections of Americana in and around Old Deerfield. Mr. Joseph Peter Spang III, associate curator of the Foundation, became an advisor to the group

* Christopher P. Monkhouse was the boy most active in forming the "American Studies Group," as they called it. The others were: Russell M. Brooks, D. Preston Goodheart, Peter A. Halstead, Osmun R. Latrobe, Robert J. McKay III, Teri N. Towe, Maurice W. Willey. Jr., and Timothy B. Wolfe.

23

Champney about 1900: a self-portrait in pastel.   *"Champ," his wife, daughter Maria, and (presumably) several friends measure*

AND THIS IS THE TOWN'S ARTIST

of inquisitive boys, and they began to meet once a week to study the village's historical collections and its colonial architecture.

The enterprise went well enough, but by the spring of 1964 the boys began to itch for a specific project to work on—something through which they could themselves make a contribution in the field of American studies. They had gradually become aware that on the walls of museums and homes in the Deerfield Valley there were a good many attractive paintings and drawings signed "Champ," or, more formally, "J. Wells

Champney," with dates ranging from the 1870's through 1900. Who was J. Wells Champney?

In a sense, answering that question, with ample illustrations, became the project the boys had been seeking. For they were not long in discovering that Champney was very much a Deerfield artist, having spent nearly all of his last thirty summers in the village, where he painted Deerfield scenes with skill and unmistakable affection. Beyond that basic fact, however, information was not so easy to come by. Champney had died in 1903, and since then had been, it seemed,

24

the elm before their Deerfield home; son Frère ignores the game.

Frère (above) and Maria, painted by their father about 1883.

As Rediscovered by Deerfield Schoolboys

largely forgotten. The boys plunged in, and by dint of many weeks of hard work, slowly assembled a mass of facts about the artist in whose life Deerfield had played such a meaningful part. But now a further project occurred to them: why not try to gather together enough Champney paintings for a full-fledged show in the Academy's Hilson Gallery?

It took a year to do it, and the co-operation of many outsiders; but by April of 1965 they were ready with a representative exhibit—more than eighty of Champney's oils, water colors, and pastels, plus many draw-

ings and photographs, loaned from museums and private homes in various parts of New England and New York. With that accomplished, Curator Spang and the boys went to work and produced an impressive illustrated catalogue including complete descriptions of the pictures in the exhibit, as well as a biographical sketch of "Champ," critical observations on his work, and a bibliography. A condensation of the biographical sketch, which was the work of Robert J. McKay, '65, appears on the following pages, and our captions draw heavily on the catalogue. —*The Editors*

25

James Wells Champney was born in Boston July 16, 1843, to James Howe Champney and his wife, Sarah Wells. When the Civil War broke out, he served in the 45th Massachusetts Volunteers for a year or more before being invalided out of the army from the effects of malaria. He then taught drawing at a "Young Ladies' Seminary" in Lexington, Massachusetts; and it was here that he met his future wife, Elizabeth Williams. From 1867 to 1869 he studied in Europe, notably under Edouard Frère, a well-known French genre painter; by 1873 he had gained some reputation as an illustrator, and was commissioned by *Scribner's Monthly Magazine* to illustrate a series of articles on the Reconstruction South. In that same year he married Miss Williams, and the couple spent a happy two years working and travelling in Europe.

In 1876 the Champneys moved into the old Wil-liams homestead in Deerfield, Mrs. Champney's an-cestral home, and Champney built his studio there. They lived in Deerfield for several years while he was professor of art at Smith College in Northampton (1877–1884), where he was one of the founders of the Art Gallery. In the summer of 1878 the artist went to Brazil to illustrate another series of articles for *Scrib-ner's*. By now the Champneys had two children, Ed-ouard Frère Champney, born in France in 1874, and Maria Mitchell Champney, born in 1877 and named for Mrs. Champney's astronomy teacher at Vassar.

In 1879 Champney opened a studio in New York City, and from that time on the Deerfield house be-came a summer home. Champney never ceased to be cosmopolitan in his habits; frequent European trips confirmed his attachment to the Old World. But his two homes, Deerfield and New York, remained the

Perhaps partly as a result of his teaching at Smith College, Champney easily established sympathetic relationships with young women, whether as art students—as at right, in one of his summer classes in Old Deerfield—or as models. The three examples opposite are from the series of twelve full-length pastels exhibited in New York in 1897 under the title, "Types of American Girlhood," modelled by well-known New York society girls. "Centuries from now," said a writer in the New York Journal, "perhaps these will be referred to for the purpose of ascertaining what the American girls at the end of the [19th] Century looked like...."

focal points of his life for both work and relaxation.

During these years Champney's artistic reputation was steadily growing. While he was teaching at Smith, the inquiries of some students had led him to work in pastels, and after 1885 he devoted himself almost exclusively to that medium. He became the foremost American pastellist of his day, well known for his numerous portraits of New York society and theatre people. He exhibited at the Philadelphia Centennial of 1876 and the Chicago Columbian Exposition of 1893; his pictures, which in earlier days he often had signed simply "Champ," were now signed "J. Wells Champney," perhaps in recognition of increased dignity.

Mrs. Champney, who was a popular children's author, often had her books illustrated by her husband, and everything indicates that the collaboration was a very happy one. Champney was an industrious and prolific painter during these years, but the limits of his profession could not circumscribe his boundless zest and curiosity. He was constantly in demand as a lecturer. He was an early and avid amateur photographer, and also used the camera as an aid to his work. He was fond of books and the theatre, was a member of a dozen clubs and artists' societies, and with Mrs. Champney entertained generously at their Fifth Avenue home and at Deerfield. "When they arrived, and Mr. Champney was seen on the street, the old town always seemed to come alive," wrote one villager.

On May 1, 1903, Champney was leaving the Camera Club in New York, when the elevator in which he was riding jammed between two floors. With typical impatience, he attempted to jump to the floor below, missed his footing, and fell down the shaft to his death. He is buried in the old cemetery in Deerfield.

ILLUSTRATIONS CONTINUED OVERLEAF

Though he worked in many mediums, and pastel ultimately became his favorite, Champney never lost his interest in the water color, which he did in a simple, lucid style. He was particularly good at rendering nuances of light; John La Farge wrote, in 1904, that in Champney's European water colors you could see "the time of day, weather, even the very different kind of light in France or England." Washing the Cans, above, is a good example of his work in water color; and also, when compared with the photograph he made of a Deerfield barn (below), it shows how useful he found the camera as an aid to authenticity in his work. He was an enthusiastic believer in photography as itself a form of art. He frequently made camera portraits of his family, photographed every canvas that he painted, and was steadily in demand to lecture on the art and technique of photography.

28

GOODBYE TO THE INTERURBAN

OR IS IT HELLO AGAIN?

By WILLIAM D. MIDDLETON

The electric cars dusted along beside dirt roads, sped through the meadows, and brought you right into Main Street. Some were little pinch-waisted wooden affairs, like the Massachusetts car at left, and some were enormous, like the one below, a relic of an unfulfilled dream called the Chicago–New York Air Line. This is an account of how, in a few brief years of glory, the interurban laced America's small towns together with a network of cheap steel rails and copper wire. The automobile, of course, brought all this to an end. Yet today the traffic is so bad that a new kind of interurban is coming back to life.

1907 CHICAGO NEW YORK AIR LINE

"Profits almost beyond calculation" prospective stockholders were promised in a series of full-page ads in Chicago newspapers one Sunday in July of 1906. Thus was launched the Chicago–New York Air Line Railroad, an interurban electric railway that would follow a straight line as nearly as was possible, said its promoters, and would whisk passengers between the two cities aboard 100-mile-per-hour trains in just ten hours, cutting eight hours off the fastest steam-train time. The Air Line was the most ambitious interurban project of them all in what, in retrospect, has been described as an era of "reckless promotion."

In all of America's transportation history there has been nothing quite like the electric interurban. An outgrowth of the urban trolley car, it first appeared only a few years before the end of the nineteenth century, and in barely two booming decades grew to a vast network reaching almost every part of the United States—and then vanished, for all practical purposes, less than half a century after it appeared.

Inventors were trying to develop electric transportation as early as 1834, when a Vermont blacksmith named Thomas Davenport operated a toy electric motor on a miniature railway. But not until 1888, when a youthful inventor named Frank J. Sprague built a twelve-mile streetcar system in Richmond, Virginia, did the electric railway really work on a large trolley system. It was quickly followed by wholesale electrification of America's horse- and cable-car lines.

A United States congressman, Charles L. Henry of Indiana, coined the word "interurban" to describe the two-mile electric line he opened in the spring of 1892 between Anderson and North Anderson, Indiana, but the fifteen-mile East Side Railway, which began operation between Portland and Oregon City, Oregon, in February of 1893, is usually regarded as the first true interurban. Others soon appeared in almost every part

TEXT CONTINUED ON PAGE 66
ILLUSTRATIONS CONTINUED ON FOLLOWING PAGES

Constructing an interurban was not a difficult task. On a still-uneven new roadbed above, workmen on an improvised tower car string wire. This was the beginning of the Oneonta, Cooperstown & Richfield Springs Railway, which began operations in 1900, a fifty-three-mile rural New York route that once boasted the elegance of parlor-car service. The line gave up passengers in 1932 and folded up in 1940.

OVERLEAF: *All the joys of a rural trolley ride are summed up in this picture of an excursion in an open car on the Bennington & Woodford, a nine-mile ride to an amusement center in Vermont. The line opened in 1895, and was washed out forever in a flood in 1898. The motorman poses with one hand on the controller handle, the other on a stem-winder hand brake; behind him on the front bench is the more daring element, which doesn't mind having its hair blown, or swallowing a few bugs as the car rushes forward.*

32

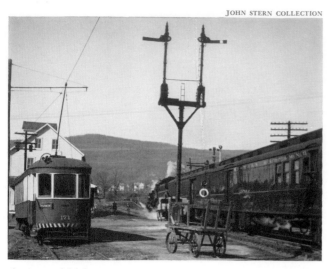

A meet with the steam cars: A car on the defunct Hagers-town & Frederick waits at the depot in Thurmont, Md.

Off to the amusement park: Double-deckers were rare, es-pecially as trailers. This one trundles through Elmira, N.Y.

Meeting the steamboat, this Spokane and Inland Empire three-car train halts on the pier at Coeur d'Alene, Idaho.

At the Lockport, New York, station, a wooden interurban of the International Railway (note baggage section) swings around the circle about 1900. The company also served Niagara Falls.

Hill and dale alike resounded to the roar of the interurban and the cry of its air horn. The bridge at left, rising some 156 feet over a ravine, was the highest on any interurban, and the heavy steel car was racing from Fort Dodge to Des Moines, Iowa. At right, an interurban of the Connecticut Company, which once ran nearly all the many electric lines in that state, travels across a salt meadow en route from Short Beach on Long Island Sound to New Haven. This stretch of track still exists, as part of the line of the Branford Electric Railway Museum, and carries passengers. Enthusiasts are presently raising funds to restore tracks beyond trestle where the car is passing.

PHOTOS BY BRUCE ROBERTS

One cold, dark winter day in 1948, trolley No. 321 made the last run on a semi-interurban that stretched through Westchester County just above New York City, with which the line was connected for many years. The red and cream cars were the same as those which plied Third Avenue, Broadway, and other Manhattan streets, but this route ran from Yonkers to Mount Vernon and New Rochelle. On the last day, No. 321 was draped in black, lettered with a lugubrious jest (see above), and escorted through various streets by police, firemen, and other dignitaries. Behind followed large, ugly buses, emitting smog. Next day, Bruce Roberts, who had seen the parade, went to the trolley graveyard near Mount Vernon and photographed the real end of No. 321 and her sisters (right) on New York's last interurban.

40

Was America the Wonderful

How many men, from how many
nations, voyaged to the American
continents before Columbus?
Norsemen certainly, around 1000 A.D.
Possibly other Europeans, by
design or accident. And, it seems quite
likely, a Buddhist named Hwui Shan,
in 458 A.D. He left a written
record. After the ludicrous uproar
last October over the Vinland Map
(which we published jointly with the
Yale University Press) it seems wise
to remind the ethnically sensitive
that this is not a new story, although
modern archaeological studies in
Mexico seem to be adding new
evidence to back up old conjectures.

Hwui Shan may have reached America in an
elaborate junk like one of these. They date
from the seventh century A.D., but even earlier
the Chinese were noted for their boatbuilding.

Hwui Shan's voyage from China, five hundred years before Leif Ericson and a thousand before Columbus, has been almost totally ignored by modern American historians, yet a rather considerable number of learned papers, articles, and even books were once written about him by Western scholars who believed that he crossed the Pacific and landed on the west coast of this continent—which he described as the wonderful Land of Fusang—in the year 458. The great Alexander von Humboldt called him the Leif Ericson of China, and the Land of Fusang the Vinland of the West. The French sinologues de Guignes and Paravey believed that he reached California. The German Karl Friedrich Neumann identified the Land of Fusang as Mexico. One American, Charles G. Leland, wrote a monograph called *Fusang* (London, 1875). Another, Edward P. Vining, compiled an 800-page encyclopaedic volume about the man he regarded as *An Inglorious Columbus* (New York, 1885). Dr. Charles E. Chapman, in his *History of California: The Spanish Period* (New York, 1921), devoted a chapter to him entitled "The Chinese Along the Pacific Coast in Ancient Times."

Hwui Shan, whose name (also written as "Hoei Shin") means "very intelligent" in Chinese, was a *cha-men,* or mendicant Buddhist priest, from Afghanistan who first came to China as a very young missionary about the year 450. The period was one of great expansion for Buddhism, and extraordinary journeys made by *cha-men* on land and sea were not at all uncommon. This one seems to have left China almost immediately, in the company of four fellow priests, on a missionary journey to evangelize new lands. His report indicates that they sailed northeast of Japan to the Land of Ta-Han (the Kamchatka Peninsula in Siberia) and from there travelled 20,000 li (about 6,600 miles) east to the Land of Fusang. This distance and direction suggest that they went by a coasting, island-hopping route across the North Pacific, past the Aleutian Islands to Alaska, and down the west coast of America as far as Mexico. There, apparently, they remained for forty years, observing the country, its people, its customs, crafts, plants, and animals—and diffusing Buddhism among the inhabitants.

At that period in Europe the Roman Empire was still in existence, and France and Germany, still

Land of Fusang?

By ROBERT LARSON

known as Gaul, were peopled by tribes of Goths. No one, as far as is known, had ever attempted—at least deliberately—to cross the mysterious ocean named for Atlantis, whose ancient civilization and disappearance had been related by Egyptian priests. Old myths and legends have given rise, of course, to the idea that there were prehistoric or very early crossings of the Atlantic. The Greeks believed that there were Isles of the Blest far out in the Western Sea inhabited by men to whom the gods had given the gift of immortality. A strangely similar paradise was known in Welsh mythology as Avalon, the abode of deathless heroes like King Arthur. Seafaring tales of great antiquity, which may or may not have been true, intermixed with fables, also contribute to the speculation that the New World may have often been found. Diodorus of Sicily said that the Phoenicians (expert seamen 1,500 years before Christ) venturing out beyond the Pillars of Hercules on their circumnavigation of Africa were blown by a storm to a large, fertile, prosperous land in the west, whose citizens enjoyed much leisure time. The historian Plutarch also recorded the yarn of certain sailors who landed in Spain circa 60 B.C. after visiting, so they said, two large Atlantic islands 10,000 *stadia* (about 1,200 miles) west of the African coast. The Portuguese, too, had their Antilia (a name that was later applied to the West Indies), which appears as an island or a large land mass on many medieval charts and globes with cartographical exactitude midway between Lisbon and Japan. In addition there was Saint Brendan (484–577), an Irish monk believed by many writers to have discovered America. There seems no doubt that he and his crew of forty other religious seafarers in their specially constructed skin-covered kayak made it to Iceland; a colony of Irish monks was found there by the Vikings when they first arrived. But even if Saint Brendan did push on for forty days and nights to the Land of the Gods, as his legend-encrusted narrative maintains, and even if it was America, Hwui Shan still preceded him by a century, for the Irishman's alleged discovery did not occur until the year 545.

After he returned to China in the year 499, Hwui Shan appeared before the Emperor Wu Ti. A kind of Marco Polo in reverse, possibly the first Oriental to have seen the West, he was then a very old man. Over-come with emotion and weeping, he presented the Emperor with gifts from the Land of Fusang and gave him a lengthy, detailed account of his travels.

It was by no means the first time the Emperor had heard of this wondrous country. Long before Hwui Shan's time Fusang was already well known to the Chinese, in poetry and fairy tale, as a kind of earthly paradise across the Pacific where everything grew to supernatural size: trees a mile high, silkworms seven feet long, birds with three legs, etcetera. In China "Fusang" is still synonymous (at least it was in pre-Communist days) with "fabulous" or "super" or "colossal." Hangchow merchants, for example, used to advertise "Fusang silk" or "Fusang porcelain," meaning something out of this world.

But *was* Fusang out of this world? Consider for a moment the thought-provoking words of one Chinese poet of the third century: *East of the Eastern Ocean lie / The shores of the Land of Fusang. / If, after landing there, you travel / East for 10,000 li / You will come to another ocean, blue, / Vast, huge, boundless.*

Behind the fiction may have been the fact of earlier discoveries and exploration. The Chinese are thought to be the first people to have developed the arts of

Could this stone head with its Oriental features be Hwui Shan or one of his companions? Made centuries before Columbus, it was found in Veracruz State, Mexico.

boatbuilding and navigation. The tall trees of the fairy tale may have been, originally, California redwoods seen by some ancient mariner from the East. Although specific evidence of a conclusive kind is lacking and no dramatic, scientifically confirmed archaeological finds have yet been made on our Pacific coast, there have been some interesting amateur discoveries. In 1882 a cache of Chinese brass coins, said to have been dated 1200 B.C., was dug up by miners at a place called Cassiar in British Columbia, along with a bronze fan bearing Chinese characters. Strange implements, believed to be Oriental, have also been unearthed in the Northwest, while Indian legends all along that coast tell of men and ships that arrived there long before the Europeans. There is, moreover, a great deal of cultural evidence of a general kind supporting the probability of ancient human contacts between Asia and America. Many arts and customs and religious beliefs of the early civilizations in Middle and South America—pictographic writing, pyramid architecture, massiveness and grotesquerie in sculpture, the belief in reincarnation, monasticism in Mexico—have definitely Oriental echoes. In an article entitled "Did Hindu Sailors Get There Before Columbus?" in *The Asia Magazine* of March 11, 1962, the modern Indian Buddhist priest Cha-men Lal presents an impressive illustrated summary of these similarities with special reference to Hinduism, the mother religion of Buddhism. "Deep in the forests of Copán in Honduras," he writes, "one may see Indra, the god of paradise in Hindu mythology, riding an elephant. Triloknath, the Hindu ruler of the three worlds, was known to the Mexicans by the same name. In a temple in Guatemala there is a statue of an incarnation of Vishnu as Kurma, the tortoise. At Copán I found no fewer than three images of Hanuman, the monkey-faced god celebrated in the Ramayana epic. How does one explain the undoubted affinity between Hinduism and the religions of South and Central America? I believe that the ancestors of the people who practised these forms of worship ventured across the Pacific Ocean as did the Malayans and the Polynesians in the fifth century, using boats much like the junks known to the Chinese."

The story of Hwui Shan, however, is unique in being the only actual record yet found that may be an historical account of such an East-West contact. There are three remarkable things about his report that strengthen the belief that he may have been our real discoverer. One is its basic historicity. It is not a work of fiction; we are not confronted here with the fantasy literature of the earlier Fusang fairy tale, but with a soberly written text preserved as such by a people who possess the oldest continuous, professionally written

history in the world. Its hero and its content have been checked by careful research and found to be congruent with other well-known persons and events. There seems to be no doubt that Hwui Shan was a real person who was thought by his contemporaries to have made a most unusual voyage east of China. On his return to King-chow he was ordered by the Emperor to tell his tale to the courtier Prince Yu Kie, who entered it in the imperial archives as one of the noteworthy happenings of the year 499. It was later published, about the year 600, by the historian Li Yan Chu, whose *Records of the Liang Dynasty* form part of the great annals of ancient China known as *The Twenty-two Historians*. Additional passages, taken from the original court archives, were published in the thirteenth century by the reputable scholar Ma Twan Lin. The story also appears or is referred to in other works of Chinese scholarship—being everywhere treated as history, not as fable—including Volume 231 of the eighteenth-century encyclopaedia *Tu-Shu-Tsi-Chin* (the Chinese invented encyclopaedias and have had them since the tenth century, one famous example, compiled in the days of the Ming Dynasty, having remained in manuscript because it was too large to print: it consisted of 22,937 books).

The second remarkable feature in Hwui Shan's story is the almost incredible accuracy of the distance and direction he gave for a journey from Asia to America, and the plausibility of his route. "Fusang is located," he said, "20,000 li east of the country of Ta Han." If you take a pair of dividers and step off this distance on a globe, figuring the Chinese li at about one-third of a mile, and follow a course along the coasts and islands from Kamchatka (Ta Han) past the Komandorskies and the Aleutians, then along the coast of Canada and the United States, you will end with astonishing accuracy in the neighborhood of Acapulco, the principal western seaport of Mexico. You will also see that the general direction "east" is not by any means inaccurate for such a journey. Contrary to a common misconception—created by the problem of conveniently printing a flat projection map of North America on a page—our western coastline does not run north and south but at about a forty-five degree angle toward the east; in other words, almost due southeast (see map on opposite page).

Thor Heyerdahl's adventure on the raft Kon-Tiki, and the unassisted nonstop crossing of the Pacific in 1962 by Kenichi Horie in his homemade nineteen-foot sailboat, have popularized the belief that the intercontinental sea route used by Orientals in ancient times must have extended across the South Pacific by way of Polynesia to Peru. But that route involves a

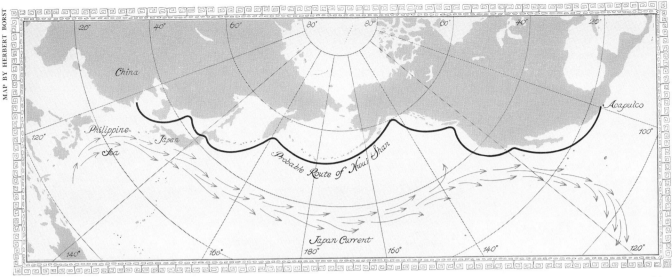

This polar projection clearly indicates how Hwui Shan could indeed have followed an easterly course to "Fusang," taking advantage of the Japan Current in the initial stages of his voyage and remaining almost continually in sight of land.

jump of more than 4,000 miles across open sea. In that era before the oceans were charted and men knew in advance where they were going, surely the North Pacific was a far more natural if not necessarily easier way to go. Asia and North America are practically joined together at Bering Strait (the classic theory regarding the origin of the American Indians is that they migrated from Asia across the land bridge that actually existed there in prehistoric times), and the sea route along the Aleutian chain is such that even a small, slow, primitive type of vessel can follow it without ever being long out of sight of land. At only one point—between the Komandorskies and the Aleutians—there is a stretch of some 200 miles of open ocean, and even there land can sometimes be seen: it has been reported that on exceptionally clear days Attu has been sighted from Siberia. At no other place in the entire archipelago are the numerous islands out of sight of each other or as much as one hundred miles apart. Frequently stormy and with few convenient landing places, this route must yet have been irresistible to ancient Asiatic mariners. A strong warm current, known as the Japan Current, or Black Stream, flows eastward along it all the way to Lower California. As it leaves Japan and passes the Kurile Islands toward Kamchatka the current reaches a speed of from seventy-five to a hundred miles a day, providing a very effective first-stage thrust for a trans-Pacific voyage. Many ships have been driven to America by the Japan Current; during the eighteenth and nineteenth centuries, when the first Europeans were starting to settle our west coast and write its history, records were made of sixty Oriental sailing vessels

that had crossed the Pacific Ocean in this way. In 1774, for instance, the Spanish explorer Juan Bautista de Anza, marching overland from Arizona to what he called "the Philippine Ocean," saw the wreck of an exotic-looking ship of non-European construction on the rocks near the Mission of Carmel. In 1815 a Japanese junk appeared off Santa Barbara with fourteen dead and three survivors on board. She had started on a simple voyage from Osaka to Tokyo, had been blown off course by a storm, and had drifted—solely by means of the current, without sail or mast or rudder—for over a year before reaching America.

Such driftings were, of course, accidental, but the Spaniards also used the Japan Current in the old days of sail. Every year for 250 years, from 1565 until 1815, the big, round-hulled Manila galleons with their broad sails and decks high on prow and stern returned to Mexico by this route from their annual journeys to Asia. Laden with 500 tons of Chinese silks and other treasures from the Orient, they sailed north from the Philippines as far as the fortieth parallel or farther to catch the current, followed it to the American coast (approximately at the present-day Oregon-California border), then continued on their way to Acapulco.

The third—and the most remarkable—quality of Hwui Shan's story is the way in which his descriptions of the people and the places he visited correspond with the North Pacific route and with what is known about America at that period. For example, he wrote: "The Land of Marked Bodies is situated 7,000 li [2,300 miles] northeast of Japan. Its people have marks [or stripes] on their bodies like wild animals. In front they have three marks. If the marks are large and

CONTINUED ON PAGE 106

One moonless spring night in 1775 a young couple crept quietly out of their house on Cornhill in Boston and ran for a waiting carriage. It bore them away through dark streets toward Boston Neck. Each moment they expected to hear a sentry's challenge, but none came and soon they were across the Charles River bound for the headquarters of the American forces at Cambridge. The young man, Henry Knox, bookseller, was one whose name appeared on Governor Gage's list of suspected rebels who must not be permitted to leave Boston; his eighteen-year-old wife was the daughter of the Royal Secretary of the Province of Massachusetts Bay. She carried her husband's sword sewn into the quilting of her cloak.

The marriage of Henry Knox to Lucy Flucker had taken place the year before and had caused a pleasurable flurry of gossip in Boston. Tory society was shocked, but the Sons of Liberty and their friends rejoiced, including an anonymous poet who celebrated the triumph of young love over parental opposition: *For who ever heard / Of a case so absurd / As a marriage deterred, / Or even deferred, / By scolding the boy / And caging the bird.*

It was indeed a mesalliance for the bride, an heiress of distinguished ancestry, raised in the heart of the Royal Governor's official world. Her father, Thomas Flucker, was an appointee of the British Crown and grandson of a founder of the town of Charlestown, across the Charles River. He lived in opulent style, his wife and daughters were ladies of fashion, and his only son was an officer in the British Army. He owned one of the first carriages imported to Boston from England (the flamboyant merchant and subsequent patriot John Hancock wrote to London to the same carriage maker to order an equipage comparable to Secretary Flucker's; namely, the best). Thomas Flucker had made two brilliant marriages, first to a Bowdoin and then to Lucy's mother, Hannah Waldo, who had inherited from her father, Brigadier Samuel Waldo, a fortune in Boston and large estates in the Province of Maine.

Henry Knox had neither fortune nor powerful ancestors. His father was an Irish immigrant who had failed as a wharf owner in Boston's South End and had departed for the West Indies, leaving Henry in charge of his younger brother, Billy, and his mother. Henry was only nine years old at the time, but he cheerfully left school and went to work for a bookselling and binding company, Messrs. Wharton and Bowes. Under the kindly eye of Nicholas Bowes, he learned to control

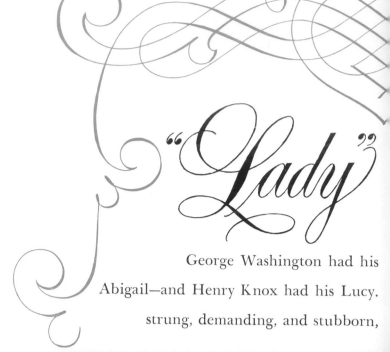

"Lady"

George Washington had his
Abigail—and Henry Knox had his Lucy.
strung, demanding, and stubborn,

MUSEUM OF FINE ARTS, BOSTON

In maturity, the Knoxes were a truly formidable couple. Gilbert Stuart's oil of Henry shows a man whose towering frame reasonably distributed his 290 pounds; Lucy (whose only known likeness is this silhouette made by a young son of

By DIANA FORBES-ROBERTSON

Knox

Martha; John Adams had his

Or did Lucy have him? She was high-

but she loved him unto death

MASSACHUSETTS HISTORICAL SOCIETY

Robert Morris, the financier) was not quite so lucky with her 250. Stuart, incidentally, who was an irascible artist, is said to have become annoyed with Knox and to have used one version of the General's portrait as a door for his pigsty.

a belligerent temper, and relinquished his position as ringleader of the South End "gang" which had a yearly brawl with the North End on "Pope's Night" when the Pope was burned in effigy. Denied the advantages of young gentlemen who drank and duelled their way through Harvard when not conning their Latin and Greek, he educated himself among his employers' books. At twenty-one he opened his own bookshop. The young gentlemen of privilege congregated there, and Henry observed their manners and soon could be mistaken for one of them.

Lucy Flucker was very fond of books and at seventeen began to join the parties of smart young people who gathered at the Knox bookstore on Cornhill, a congenial place "of great display and attraction for young and old, and a fashionable morning lounge," wrote a contemporary. The girl's interest in books was rapidly transferred to the bookseller, whom she had also seen, splendidly accoutered and mounted upon a sturdy horse, parading on Boston Common with the Grenadier Corps of the militia. Frequently the imperious, spoiled Miss Flucker led the young proprietor away from chatting groups for private talks among the bookshelves. It is said that the young man's emotions were so stirred by his charming client that he could not make correct change.

When Lucy's parents got wind of what was going on in the bookshop, they exploded in wrath. For one thing, they had no liking for a son-in-law "in trade." And what was even worse, young Knox was in sympathy with those rebellious American colonists who were making such a fuss about taxes and who that very winter had tossed tea into Boston Harbor. Although for reasons of business Henry tried to be discreet—he simulated a quarrel with his friend Paul Revere when their earnest discussion was interrupted by the arrival of a Tory in the shop—he was suspected of active participation. He had done little yet but listen, read, and debate with friends, but in his heart he had no doubts; he had been present at the Boston Massacre and had seen the redcoats fire upon the crowd.

Lucy soon made up her mind that she wanted "her Harry," and neither reason nor force would change it. Her parents tried to prevent meetings but Lucy defied them when she could; the lovers exchanged fervent letters, signing themselves "Speria" and "Fidelio." Lucy was violently emotional and inclined to hysterical scenes if crossed. She wore her parents down while Boston society watched the battle with glee. Harry was the man she wanted, a strong, positive, cheerful man who could calm her seething temperament. And

CONTINUED ON PAGE 74

47

Rescuers on the Oklahoma's *upturned hull listen for the tapping of trapped survivors, among them Seaman Young (below). In the back-*

"*God, please get us out of this*"

A carefree Sunday lay ahead for the *Oklahoma*'s mess cook. His pockets jingled, and a pretty girl awaited him for a picnic on a warm, white beach. Minutes later he lay entombed at the bottom of Pearl Harbor

By STEPHEN BOWER YOUNG

ground are the masts of the Maryland.

The world was my oyster that Sunday morning in December, 1941. I was nineteen, breakfast was over, and liberty would be starting in an hour or so. A quick look out a second-deck porthole of our battleship, the U.S.S. *Oklahoma*, confirmed my feeling that this was going to be a glorious day. There were still some early morning clouds, but the sun was warm, with just a breath of trade wind ruffling the waters of the harbor. I turned to swab down the deck around me. Someone had spilled coffee there.

I would be happy to get this three-month tour of mess-cooking over with so that I could get back on deck again. Topside had been my cleaning station for the past year, ever since I had come on board ship in Long Beach. I liked being out in the weather, scrubbing and holystoning decks, scraping and painting the bulkheads or gun-turret sides, shining brightwork, splicing line, rigging boat booms, and working at the aviation crane, aft. I had made seaman-first as soon as I was eligible and expected to make cox'n in the spring. But I often wondered whether I should strike for gunner's mate instead. The 14-inch guns in the division's massive No. 4 turret aft fascinated me. My battle station was in the upper starboard powder-hoist room where we rolled the heavy powder bags through flameproof doors into the turret chamber to feed the guns.

The *Oklahoma* was old, but she had a kind of dignity, with her broad beam and tripod masts. The home of a thousand sailors, she had never fired a gun in anger, not even in World War I. Her cruising speed was only ten knots or so, but when she left the Golden Gate behind and began to push her ponderous bulk into the Pacific swells, you could feel her strength. I was proud to be a sailor in her crew.

All non-rated hands had to take their turn as mess cooks before going up for a rate. It was compulsory, but I had managed to avoid it until I had no choice. Now, only a few more weeks remained of lugging steaming tureens of chow up and down ladders from the midship galley to the living compartment aft where the fourth deck division messed as well as slept. It always seemed a long way back and forth to our fantail hatch, a trip I made a dozen or so times a meal, not counting runs for seconds. But in a heavy sea, while balancing a tureen of soup in one hand and a platter of baked ham in the other, it seemed even longer. Setting up tables and carrying racks of dirty dishes to the scullery was no fun either, but the six of us who had the duty worked hard and made the best of it. It had been pretty easy this morning, for the boys had been on the town in Honolulu last night and were sleeping late. Everyone was up now, though, and I was anxious to make that first liberty launch ashore. One of my buddies grinned, "Don't hurry, your girl will wait."

"We're going on a picnic," I told him, as, together, we heaved up the last mess table and secured it.

49

My girl and I were going to Nana-kuli, where the surf was much better than Waikiki and the beach not nearly so crowded. For once I had plenty of money—a ten and a one-dollar bill. Nice going at fifty-four bucks a month with a week of the month already gone.

The compartment rocked with shouts and laughter—with only a muffled undertone of growls from the duty-section men who had to stay on board and derive most of their day's amusement from the Sunday funnies.

I looked at my watch. Two minutes to morning colors. I started toward my locker.

Suddenly the bugle blared over the PA system. The sound filled the compartment. The first few notes told me it was not colors or calling away a motor launch. I stopped and listened. It was the call for gun crews to man their antiaircraft stations. The word was passed, "Man the antiaircraft batteries!" Not my station, I thought. And what a crazy time to hold a drill!

"What's going on?" we asked each other. But no one knew, and we returned to whatever we had been doing.

Again the bugle tore the air. Now it was the call to general quarters! A voice boomed throughout the ship—"All hands, man your battle stations!" What the hell was this? Drills on Sunday? They knew we were all waiting to go ashore.

The harsh, excited voice on the PA system froze us in our tracks. "All hands, man your battle stations! On the double! This is no drill! Get going—they're real bombs!"

I headed for my turret battle station. Everyone was running and pushing. The ship shuddered as she was hit somewhere forward. I stumbled, but managed to stay on my feet. The lights went out just as I reached the ladder going down to the deck below. I groped my way, and as I hit the deck the emergency lights went on dimly. Another ladder to go. Another hit. Close by, this time. The deck heaved, but I hung on. The emergency lights went out momentarily. Obviously, we were being badly hit.

Finally, I made it down the ladder, slipping and sliding on the rungs following the man in front of me and avoiding the feet of the sailor behind, through the barbette and into the turret. The crew was milling around manning stations and scrambling up inside the turret to the guns above. I climbed up to the shell deck on my way to the hoist room. The officer in charge—the same one who had passed the word—ordered, "Stay below, men. Below the armored deck. These 14-inch guns are no good against planes. I'm going topside to see what's going on!" He never returned.

On the way back to the powder-handling room I stumbled over a kneeling figure, fumbling at a shoe lace. He looked up and I saw that he was crying. He was a petty officer, a real tough guy, merciless in his treatment of the crew. I moved on.

The powder-handling room was crowded. Indistinctly I could see the faces of my friends, frightened, anxious, and unbelieving. Standing against the bulkhead, I grabbed for support as another hit made the deck beneath us jump. Until now, we supposed they were bombs, and felt almost safe below the armored deck. No one had thought yet of torpedoes tearing away a ship's side.

Then someone yelled and pointed to a spot where water was pouring in through the lower portside bulkhead. The ship was listing slightly. Horrified, we watched the water rise and felt the deck slipping from under us as the list became more pronounced. Gear of all descriptions commenced to tumble about, and sailors began to scramble for the ladder leading upward. "All our breakfast dishes must be breaking!" I blurted. There was some nervous laughter from the few who knew I was a mess cook. "Don't laugh," I said. "They'll take it out of my pay."

We tried to get up the ladder to the next deck above. A few men attempted to wriggle up through an emergency escape tube which was only two or

three feet wide. But it was useless; they got stuck before they could make it out. I raised my head above the shell-deck level just as the *Oklahoma*'s enormous shells, weighing a ton apiece, broke loose from their moorings and rolled wildly down the slanting deck where sailors were fighting to stay on their feet. There was no possible escape for these men, and I recoiled from the terrible sights and sounds.

Ducking back down into the handling room, I shouted, "They're just counterflooding to get us back on an even keel so they can fire the guns." This information seemed to calm the men for a few moments, but as the list increased, their excitement mounted. Sailors fell down the deck and met their deaths violently. Numbly I watched two friends of mine, arms and legs waving wildly, as they and the gear which had knocked them off their feet smashed into the debris at the bottom of the slanting deck. By the faint light I could see that they had joined others—floating face down in the water.

I clutched at the bulkhead, barely able to stay on my feet as the water flooded in. That was when the dreaded phrase was passed from man to man throughout the ship, "Abandon ship! Abandon ship!"

More shells broke loose. I could see them coming and yelled to a cox'n friend across the tilting deck, who was hanging onto the powder hoist, "Catch me! I'm coming over!" It was terribly clear to me that if he were unable to catch me, or if I were to lose my grip, I would slide helplessly down the deck and be slammed into the farther bulkhead either to drown or be crushed by those shells.

Desperately, I leaped across the space between us. He caught my outstretched

The remains of "Battleship Row" three days after the attack. At right are the capsized Oklahoma *and the* Maryland. *At center are the* West Virginia *(awash) and the* Tennessee. *Astern, with only her masts and turrets above water, is the* Arizona, *aboard which over 1,000 died.*

arm as I vaulted from the path of the rolling shells. I think I thanked him as I grabbed the powder hoist and hung on. Looking up, I saw the head and shoulders of a sailor hanging upside down from the hatch above. His arms hung limply, swaying slightly. I had known him. We had gone through training together in Newport, played baseball there and in the Fleet. I looked away from his inverted eyes.

We could not get out. We were being hit again and again, dreadful, tearing hits. We realized all at once that these were not bombs, but torpedoes. And the ship was wide open, no watertight integrity at all. Every compartment, every void space, was open to the sea once the hull was torn apart. It had never happened that way before that I could remember, but there was an inspection scheduled for the next day and all spaces had been ordered opened.

The list rapidly increased until it seemed that the ship was almost lying on her side. With awful certainty we knew that we were sinking. Suddenly the ship lurched! The deck slipped out from under me and my hands snatched at empty air. As she rolled over, I was pitched into a mass of dead and dying and, with them, buffeted and tossed about. Then the dark waters closed over me as the ship came to rest upside down on the bottom of the harbor.

Eventually I surfaced, gulped for air, and swam desperately in the darkness, surprised to find myself alive. Random shouts mingled with cries for help; then quiet fell abruptly. Water gurgled as it made its way into the ship. I thought we were done for.

Suddenly, a voice I recognized cried, "Help! I can't swim!"

Someone switched on a battle lantern. It still worked, thank heaven. The light shone eerily in the darkness. The handling room was a shambles. Loose gear and dead bodies were floating everywhere.

I swam to the man who had called and grabbed him by the hair to hold

him above water. An opening was spotted leading to a passageway, and we all swam for the hatch with my friend safely in tow. We gained the passageway and found it was only partly full of water. A hasty head count showed thirty of us huddled there.

I volunteered to take a look around and jumped along a half-submerged ladder to take the lantern. "It's a good thing this has waterproof batteries," I observed. "Everybody knows how dependable they are." We smiled a little, remembering magazine advertisements and illustrations of people in tough spots who were saved by their trusty flashlights. "Don't go away," I added, "I'll be back." No one said anything except that they knew there was no way out.

Taking a deep breath, I ducked under water, reached another compartment, and surfaced. Flashing the light around, I saw that I was in a flooded living compartment. It was difficult to orient myself. There should be a porthole or escape hatch here, but I could see nothing except floating mattresses and bodies. When I finally found a porthole, there was a body stuck in it, a plump body. I grabbed the feet and yanked, but couldn't budge him. The irony of it! Slim as I was, I could have made it through. Everything else was blocked and jammed. I found my way back to the passageway and broke the bad news to the men.

Other areas were investigated, but we found no way out. We were in a pocket of air that had been trapped as the ship went down. Although our space was only partially flooded, we knew it was simply a matter of time until the air gave out and the water took over. It was rising slowly. We settled back to wait. Rescue seemed neither probable nor possible. I was sure that if the Navy could rescue us, it would. But by now, for all we knew, the Japs might have taken over Pearl Harbor anyway. The situation seemed hopeless.

"No talking," ordered a voice out of the dark. "We've got to save the air."

CONTINUED ON PAGE 109

Among those who came to the aid of the Union when the Civil War broke out was François Ferdinand Philippe Louis Marie, Prince de Joinville, the third son of the exiled King of France, Louis Philippe. The Prince was doubly gifted, as both soldier and artist. AMERICAN HERITAGE herewith presents the story of his visit, recounted by a distinguished French novelist and essayist, along with a portfolio of the Prince's water colors. Both recently appeared in a limited edition of *A Civil War Album of Paintings by the Prince de Joinville*; together they give a fresh, behind-the-lines glimpse of an ill-prepared nation fighting for its life.

By ANDRÉ MAUROIS
of the Académie Française

A Princely Service

On October 15, 1862, in Paris, an article was published in the *Revue des Deux Mondes* on "The Campaign of the Army of the Potomac." The article was signed "A. Trognon," and it summarized, the *Revue* stated, the notes "of an officer who took part in the recent battles in Virginia." Actually Trognon was a pseudonym, and the Prince de Joinville, the third son of King Louis Philippe, was the real author. Emperor Napoleon III ruled in France at that time, and a member of the dethroned royal [Orleanist] family was not authorized to sign an article, especially on such a subject. However, after the fall of the Empire in 1870, when the *Revue* published an Index of all the texts included between 1831 and 1874, the Prince de Joinville found his name there. . . .

Why did Joinville, his son, the Duc de Penthièvre, and his nephews, the Comte de Paris and the Duc de Chartres, put themselves at the disposal of the North during the War of Secession? There were two reasons. First of all they were liberals sincerely opposed to slavery. But they also suffered from the inactivity to which their exile had condemned them. Soldiers at heart, they wanted to fight. They were not permitted to fight for France. At least, while fighting for Lincoln, they would learn the use of new techniques in modern warfare. The Prince de Joinville had been an excellent admiral; so we can imagine how interested he was in the naval blockade, the new ironclad ships, and the landing operations. He could even give sound advice.

He arrived in 1861 after the defeat of the first Battle of Bull Run. The Confederate Army camped within sight of Washington. The cannon roared. In the midst of this excitement the Army of the Potomac was born. . . . For a long time Washington had hoped that "everything would work out." The North felt the stronger because of its potential and its population, and thought it was useless "to go to trouble in advance." After Bull Run all illusions were dissipated. . . .

The Prince observed the Northerners' lack of military organization. . . . [He believed] the North relied too much on volunteers. Joinville, a professional soldier, thought that 60,000 regular troops would be more effective than three times as many volunteers.

"In America, however," he wrote, "they do not know that, and what is more, they do not want to know it. That would be repudiating their deeply rooted belief that every American, when he wants something, finds himself equal to the task without previous training, and that consequently there is no volunteer who, on donning the uniform, does not assume simultaneously the qualities of a soldier. In addition the officers of West Point are considered aristocrats simply because they recognize the necessity of a hierarchy. And everything that is aristocratic is bad." To give much power to a professional army, the Northerners thought, would be to jeopardize their liberties. One cannot make a *coup d'état*, they said, with volunteers.

That, added Joinville, is understood, but neither is it easy to make an army of volunteers victorious. The regiments are raised by men who insist on commanding them, "and there is Mr. So-and-so, a doctor or a lawyer, who, without having ever touched a sword, becomes a colonel straight away . . . Then there is the problem of finding soldiers; it is difficult, for there is a great deal of competition." One comes to an agreement with a few friends, imbued with the martial spirit, who promise to bring a certain number of recruits if this one will be commissioned captain, that one, lieutenant. The Catholic priests are approached "to get some Irishmen." The soldiers have no illusions about these improvised officers. "They don't know any more about it than we do," they said, hence a lack of discipline and respect.

Just as the French princes arrived, Lincoln was trying to correct these serious deficiencies in his army; but he refused, like his adversary, Jefferson Davis, to resort to conscription. Far from blaming him, Joinville praised him: "If it was his duty to repress a revolt, the President did not want, except in the case of absolute necessity, to interfere in the rights that, until then, had made the American people the happiest, and at the same time, the freest people on earth." * Here one

* In the spring of 1862, the Confederate congress passed a conscription act. The Federal government passed a similar act the following year.—*Ed.*

sees the liberalism of the Princes of Orléans. Two of them, the Comte de Paris and the Duc de Chartres, had been attached to the staff of McClellan, the commander in chief. Joinville, on the other hand, remained a civilian observer and counselor.

He got along well with McClellan. "Little Mac" reminded him of Bonaparte because of his youth, his love of letters, his small stature, and his hand in his frock coat. He was admired and even worshipped by his soldiers. The general plan to follow seemed simple to Joinville. There could be no question of conquering and occupying the immense territory of the South. But through a blockade the navy could succeed in isolating this region effectively. It captured New Orleans and blockaded the Mississippi on April 25, 1862. "That was the most important thing," said Admiral de Joinville; "in this way we put the key in our pocket." As for the Army of the Potomac, its objective was to drive the Confederates from Richmond. . . .

In Washington the more timid said: "But the enemy is still across the river from the city in Manassas and Centreville. If the army withdraws, Washington will be in danger." On the evening of March 9, 1862, a friend tapped the Prince de Joinville on the shoulder: "Don't you know? The enemy has evacuated Manassas and the army is leaving tomorrow." Joinville sketched brilliantly, both in drawing and in writing. Here is his version of the departure: "The next day, in fact, the whole city of Washington was in a commotion. A mass of artillery, cavalry, and wagons filled the streets, moving toward the bridges over the Potomac. On the sidewalks one could see officers tenderly bidding adieu to their ladies in tears. The civilian population dispassionately watched them leave. There was a marked absence of enthusiasm. Perhaps it was the fault of the rain that fell in torrents."

In the midst of the batteries . . . he met General McClellan on horseback, worried, riding off alone, without aides. "Anyone who could have seen into the general's soul that day would have detected the bitterness that was later to accumulate there so cruelly." There was no lack of cause for bitterness. For a long time McClellan had been preparing to make a crossing to the Virginia Peninsula. Opening the campaign had been imposed on him unseasonably. His superiors reproached him for not having attacked the badly defended positions at Manassas and for letting himself be intimidated by wooden cannons, and even by a stovepipe that looked like a cannon. Joinville defended him: "McClellan knew better than anyone what to expect from the forces that occupied Manassas and Centreville, but he also knew that until April the Virginia roads would be in such a state that it would only be possible to move transport and cannons by building

wooden roads, an arduous task. . . ." [Since assuming command of the Northern troops on July 27, 1861, McClellan had been hard at work in Washington creating a new national army to replace the ninety-day militia regiments which had made up the bulk of the Northern forces in the first months of the war. Joinville obviously approved of his professionalism. McClellan did not want to move against Richmond until he felt that his army was ready, but his caution brought charges of cowardice and even disloyalty from the radical Republicans. On March 11, 1862, Lincoln relieved McClellan of supreme command of the Northern forces. He was left in command of the Army of the Potomac and ordered to begin operations against Richmond at once.]

Whatever the case, McClellan was severely attacked. When forced to explain his plans, he submitted them; and the next day they were known to the enemy, doubtlessly informed, Joinville said, "by those thousands of female agents who spy for him even in the most intimate nooks." Should they march overland to Richmond or continue with the landing plan for which the ships were not yet assembled? Joinville considered pursuit overland impossible. Taking into consideration the requirements of the American soldier and the enormousness of his rations, as well as the need to bring everything into an area where nothing was to be found, the army could subsist only by relying on the railroads or navigable waterways. Since the enemy had rendered the railways impracticable, it was necessary to resort to transportation by water. . . . [McClellan rejected the plan to move against Richmond overland via Manassas, and decided to go down to Fort Monroe on Hampton Roads by steamboat and then advance up the Virginia Peninsula, using the rivers for supply and communication. His army began embarking from Alexandria, Virginia, on March 17.]

Joinville's naval talents now come to the forefront: "In the West the Union armies marched from success to success thanks to the support of the navy; in the East the contrary was true. One single sea battle in Confederate waters was perhaps going to paralyze the Federal army. . . . How true it is that experience has not yet taught even the most powerful seafaring nations the great advantage to be gained in land warfare from a well-organized navy!" [Union gunboats had played a major role in the capture of Forts Henry and Donelson in Tennessee in February; a month later they were decisive in the fall of the Confederate strongpoints of New Madrid, Missouri, and Island Number Ten, Tennessee, in the Mississippi. But the appearance of the Confederate ironclad *Merrimac* at Hampton Roads on March 8 threw the North into a panic.]

When the march toward the enemy lines finally be-

TEXT CONTINUED ON PAGE 80
ILLUSTRATIONS CONTINUED ON FOLLOWING PAGES

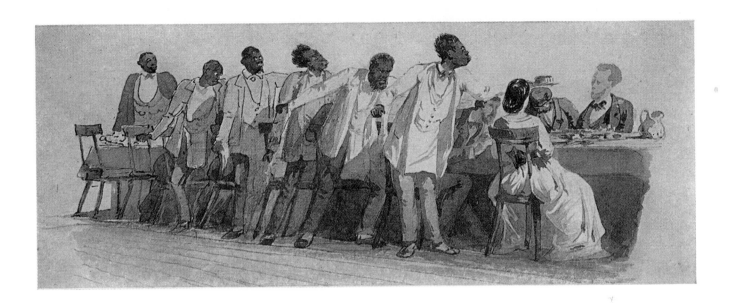

THE SKETCHBOOK OF THE
Prince de Joinville

In the year that the Prince de Joinville was in America as an observer with the Federal forces, he made an engaging visual record of what he saw. In more than fifty water colors and sketches he vividly captured the foibles and heroism of the Americans, recorded the beauties of the landscape and the ugliness of war, and caught the Union soldier in moments of action and repose. It would be difficult to pay a better tribute to the artistic skill of the Prince than did his friend General McClellan in his memoirs: "The Prince de Joinville sketched admirably and possessed a most keen sense of the ridiculous, so that his sketchbook was an inexhaustible source of amusement, because everything ludicrous that struck his fancy on the march was sure to find a place there. He was a man of far more than ordinary ability and of excellent judgment." This sense of the ridiculous, as well as his ability as a water-colorist, is admirably revealed in the picture above. Though there is some doubt as to whether the dinner portrayed ever actually took place, there is a ring of truth to Joinville's depiction of the Negro waiters fighting to serve President and Mrs. Lincoln while the other guests dodge the proffered food. The Prince did in fact meet Lincoln soon after arriving in this country, and most of his other water colors are of scenes he himself witnessed. This and the others on the next six pages were chosen from the collection of his great-grandson, Monseigneur le Comte de Paris, by whose special permission they are reproduced here.
                                                                    —*The Editors*

As a visitor from abroad, the Prince de Joinville had the advantage of seeing American army life with a fresh and often humorous eye. Above left, a Union soldier is forced to wear a barrel and to tiptoe through the regimental area, a humiliating punishment usually reserved for petty thieves and stragglers; it was sometimes followed by the offender's being drummed out of the Army. At lower left, a treetop sentinel guards a picnic of civilians, Union officers, and their hoop-skirted ladies. And below, a teamster, his hat set squarely on his head, rides one of his horses, while in the wagon a soldier, the epitome of all war weariness, snatches some sleep. Above is a water color the Prince made of his nephews, the Comte de Paris and the Duc de Chartres, at a Federal army camp early in the spring of 1862. Joinville had originally intended to send the picture home to relatives in Europe as a kind of record of life in the United States Army, but he afterward changed his mind, and the water color remained in his sketchbook.

The Prince de Joinville's ability to depict character is most evident in these water colors of Union leaders. His picture of General George McClellan (left), the commander of the Army of the Potomac, dictating an order during the Peninsular Campaign of April–May, 1862, makes it perfectly clear why McClellan's foes said he was "the only man ever born who can strut sitting down." Behind McClellan stand General R. B. Marcy (with the white mustache), his Chief of Staff and father-in-law, and General Fitz-John Porter, a corps commander.

Officers and Gentlemen

General Andrew Porter, Provost Marshal of the Army of the Potomac, (above) was noted for his harshness to Union military offenders and Confederate prisoners and for his unsympathetic attitude toward the Negroes who sought refuge with the Northern troops. Joinville depicts all of these characteristics in his picture of the fat, pompous Porter mounted on his beautiful horse, while a Negro cringes before him and a provost guard sneers behind his back. George Armstrong Custer (left), a young aide-de-camp fresh out of West Point, was a highly individualistic dresser; to Joinville, a stickler for correct military form, the result was a highly unsoldierly appearance. This unflattering rear view of Custer shows him wearing a peculiar hat, sagging boots, and baggy pants. In sharp contrast is the portrait of General George Stoneman (right), Chief of Cavalry of the Army of the Potomac. Stoneman, a superb officer and a favorite of the Prince, seems to sum up all that is meant by the phrase "correct military bearing."

Gal Stoneman.

Like any soldier, Joinville knew that war was indeed hell, but two separate hells—one of fear, the other of boredom. Above, a lone Union cannoneer sits beside his bronze 12-pounder, which is pointed down the main road leading from Washington to Richmond. He sits and waits for an attack that will probably never come. For though there was a great deal of fear for the safety of Washington, the city was heavily fortified soon after the war broke out and the Confederates tried only once—in July of 1864—to break through the ring of guns. They were repulsed. At the right the hell of fear is expressed in every muscle of the soldiers ducking a Southern shell zooming toward their entrenchments during the Union siege of Yorktown in the spring of 1862. Most of the soldiers are wearing the French Zouave uniform, popular with both Yankee and Rebel troops. It is just one indication—the kepi is another—of the pervasive influence of French military ideas in the Civil War. At a time when Napoleon Bonaparte was judged to have been the greatest general of all time, and the current Emperor of France, Napoleon III, was making his army the model for the world, French military tactics and equipment were considered supreme. At West Point, where almost all of the top commanders of both sides were trained, Dennis Hart Mahan was one of the most influential members of the faculty. He was, among other things, professor of "the Art of War" and had spent four years in France studying French military methods. One of the textbooks used in his course was Baron Henri Jomini's An Abstract of the Art of War. Jomini, a Swiss who had participated in the Napoleonic campaigns, was carefully studied by the military leaders of the North and South and even by Lincoln. One of his strategic ideas—that it was necessary to capture the enemy's capital—did much to create the Union cry of "On to Richmond!" Other French military concepts were popular in the Civil War: the formation of infantrymen into hollow squares for defense and the employment of masses of artillery. And the most widely used fieldpiece of the war, the 12-pound smoothbore like the one in the painting above, was called a "napoleon," after Napoleon III.

War Is
Hell,
Sometimes

A
Keen
Student
of
Tactics

62

Joinville was fascinated by the highly mobile character of the American Civil War, particularly by the tactical employment of cavalry. In the picture at left, he depicted a mounted Union patrol questioning a runaway slave near Worktown, Virginia, as to the size and location of nearby Confederate forces. (The slaves were of some help in providing information, but, as Joinville wrote in his journal, they "generally told us much more than they knew in order to secure a welcome, and we had no maps and no knowledge of localities. It was impossible to make anything of their stories, and to reconcile their often contradictory statements.") In the picture below, Joinville painted an encounter between Union and Confederate cavalry patrols somewhere in Virginia in December of 1861. Inside the house, a group of Southerners fire at the Yankees, while Union reinforcements gallop up from the trees beyond. The use of cavalry by such masters of the strategic raid as the Southerners J. E. B. Stuart and Nathan Bedford Forrest and the Northerner Judson Kilpatrick made a strong impression on Joinville; he also included in his sketchbook pictures of ironclads and of railroads being used for military purposes. Indeed, his is the record of a man who realized that, in numbers of men engaged, distances covered, and techniques employed, the American Civil War was unlike any war before it. The conflict had not continued very long before most of the generals of Europe agreed with Joinville, and by 1864 the great powers—France, Prussia, and England—had sent observers to study every detail of the unfolding spectacle.

FACES FROM THE PAST—XX

"On the whole," wrote the drama critic of the Chicago *Times* of the show that opened on December 16, 1872, "it is not probable that Chicago will ever look upon the like again. Such a combination of incongruous drama, execrable acting, renowned performers, mixed audience, intolerable stench, scalping, blood and thunder, is not likely to be vouchsafed to a city for a second time,—even Chicago." The play, *The Scouts of the Plains*, had as its principals "Buffalo Bill" Cody and "Texas Jack" Omohundro (a former scout with Jeb Stuart's cavalry), both playing themselves; Mlle. Morlacchi, acting the part of Dove Eye (she was described by the *Tribune*'s critic as "a beautiful Indian maiden with an Italian accent and a weakness for scouts"); numerous supers as Indian warriors; and the man known as Ned Buntline, in whose wildly fertile imagination the spectacle had originated, playing the hero, Cale Durg. (He is posing, opposite, in costume for that role.) In city after city in which the troupe performed, critics carped. The New York *Herald* said that Buntline played the part of Cale Durg "as badly as is possible for any human being to represent it," and took particular exception to the scene in which Durg, momentarily subdued by redskins, was tied to a tree with a torture fire ignited at his feet, from which position he delivered a long temperance lecture. But with the public, Ned Buntline had scored again.

Born in 1823 as Edward Zane Carroll Judson (on a night, he later wrote, "when thunder loudly booming/shook the roof above my head—/When red lightning lit the glooming /Which o'er land and sea was spread"), he ran away to sea when he was eleven, embarking upon a career in which fact and fiction became so thoroughly entangled as to defy separation. By the time he was twenty he had fought in the Seminole War, taken his first wife, and published his first story—under the pseudonym Ned Buntline (a buntline being a rope at the bottom of a square sail). Before long he had, by his own account, travelled to the Far West and killed buffaloes and grizzlies; started a periodical called *Ned Buntline's Own*; and been lynched in Nashville, Tennessee. There, shortly after his wife died, Ned had made no secret of his admiration for young Mrs. Robert Porterfield, and one day her husband came looking for him. Porterfield fired at Buntline, who took aim and shot his pursuer through the head. Ned was in court pleading self-defense when Porterfield's brother and some friends poured in and started shooting. After a wild chase, during which Ned was hit in the chest by one bullet, he fell forty-seven feet from a window (the injury left him with a limp for life) and was captured by the sheriff's men. That night a mob stormed the jail, dragged him from his cell, and strung him up by the neck from a post on Public Square. But Ned had one of those miraculous escapes so familiar to readers of the stories he would write: three weeks later a letter from his cell reported that he would be leaving soon; after complaining of the gross injustice done him, he noted that the "rope didn't break, it was cut by a friend."

Back in the East, he resumed publication of *Ned Buntline's Own*, began cranking out paperback books that sold for ten cents (dime novels, people called them), and embarked upon a social reform series entitled *The Mysteries and Miseries of New York*. It was "drawn from *life*," he wrote, "heart-sickening, *too-real* life"—a life full of clerks who had embezzled money to pay their debts, only to find themselves in the toils of gamblers; of proud but poor sewing girls, fighting off tuberculosis and libertines ("By Jove, I'll have a kiss if I die for it!" "Wretch! Fiend! *dog!* Back, sir! stand back, if you value your life!"). And so on, from one insoluble dilemma to another, with hero and heroine on the brink of destruction or ruin or both at the end of each installment. *The Mysteries and Miseries* sold over 100,000 copies, and reprints and translations made Ned Buntline a sub-literary figure of world renown. Married again now, he explained to his latest bride that he kept a sword, pistols, and a dagger in his study because his life was in constant danger from the villains he was exposing.

Between stories and issues of *Ned Buntline's Own*, he found time to get into an unending variety of scrapes and scandals. Once, while out of jail on bond pending trial in a riot case, he was served with summonses in a slander suit and a divorce, and was arrested for debt. He became involved in spiritualism, labored mightily for the Know-Nothing party, organized a concert troupe, was arrested in St. Louis for leading a riot, gave temperance lectures (many of them while drunk), shot at least one man, and married several women (at least two concurrently), was jailed for bigamy, served in the Civil War (he later claimed that he was a "chief of scouts with the rank of colonel"), and produced an endless number of books—*The Boot-Maker of Fifth Avenue, or, A Fortune from Petroleum; Merciless Ben, the Hair Lifter; Quaker Saul, the Idiot Spy, or, Luliona, the Seminole: A Tale of Love, Strife & Chivalry; Thayendanegea, the Scourge, or, the War-Eagle of the Mohawks: A Tale of Mystery, Ruth, and Wrong;* and so on and on.

In 1869, while on a trip to the West, Ned Buntline met the tall, good-looking plainsman named William Cody, and it was only a matter of months before Cody had become "Buffalo Bill, The King of Border Men," hero of a new Buntline series. Then Ned persuaded Cody to join him in Chicago to perform in *The Scouts of the Plains*. Ned took just four hours to write the play, rehearsed it twice, and it ran for more than two years—two years during which Buffalo Bill became a national hero, symbol of all that was bravest and best on the frontier. Ned Buntline lived on until 1886, turning out stories until the last, but of all his characters, only the greatest—Buffalo Bill—survived him for long.

—*Richard M. Ketchum*

of the United States, and by the turn of the century the boom was on.

It seemed to be just what America was waiting for. Local intercity service on the steam railroads was usually slow and infrequent, and the Model T and paved highways were still a few decades away. Frequent service was easy to provide on the interurban, for one car made a train. Fares were almost always lower than steam-road rates. Convenience was still another important factor, for the interurbans stopped almost anywhere, and usually operated into the heart of town over city streets, something that was to doom them in later years.

Travel by interurban was an experience virtually impossible to duplicate today. An infinitely more impressive and elegant vehicle than the city streetcar from which it grew, the interurban car was an imposing sight as it worried its way through the traffic of city streets, bound for the countryside and its own private rails. Once free of the city the big cars sped along at exhilarating speeds, swaying and nosing from side to side on the often uneven track. Windows flung open against the warmth of a summer's day caught the rich odors of the countryside, sometimes mingled with the ozone smell generated by the electric traction motors or the pungent odor of grinding brake shoes as the car slowed for a stop. There was a high-pitched screaming from the traction motors and gears, and periodically the air compressor beneath the car cut in with its characteristic *lung-a-lung-a-lung*. The conductor's signal cord, suspended from the ceiling, flip-flopped back and forth, and there was a muffled creaking from the car's ornate woodwork.

A hissing sound from the overhead trolley wire and the rising clatter of its wheels over rail joints signalled the approach of the interurban, and a wailing air horn brought cross traffic to an abrupt halt at a respectful distance from the track. A massive arc headlight and a wooden cowcatcher of imposing size gave the onrushing interurban a commanding presence. Trackside vegetation bent aside in the breeze, and dust clouds rose from road crossings as the electric car sped by in varnished, Gothic-windowed majesty. At night, particularly when the overhead wire was coated with sleet, the countryside was illuminated with great blue flashes every time the racing trolley wheel, or shoe, momentarily lost contact with the wire.

Inside the car, passengers reclined in roomy, plush-

or leather-upholstered ease. Carpeted floors were common in some of the more elegant cars, and, on the longer runs, travellers were sometimes treated to buffet-parlor cars, fitted with wicker lounge chairs and equipped with small kitchens from which à la carte meals were served. A few of the longer lines even provided sleeping-car service.

There was an easy informality about interurban travel. Most of the train crews knew their regular clientele on a first-name basis, and they were not above such homely tasks as running a few errands for a housewife along the line, or making a special stop and seeing to the safe arrival of an unescorted child at his destination. The baggage compartment up front was usually piled high with a mélange of express parcels, milk cans, crated baby chicks, and mail bags. On a few of the more important runs the cars even boasted a full-fledged Railway Post Office compartment.

In the earlier years the two-man crew was almost universal. The blue-uniformed, brass-buttoned conductor collected fares, chatted with the passengers, and in the wintertime—if the car wasn't equipped with electric heaters—stoked the coal stove that kept the interior comfortably overheated. Meanwhile the motorman, sealed off in his special compartment, busied himself with the electric controller, air brakes, and air horn. The title "motorman" was almost universal on the interurbans, but a few lines favored the steam roads' more pretentious "engineer." One line, the Puget Sound Electric, couldn't make up its mind which to use and finally compromised on "motoneer." In later years, as an economy move, many lines adopted cars that could be operated by a single man.

Usually interurban lines were quickly and cheaply built. The industry grew prodigiously, if not always

At the height of the interurban era a buff could ride all the way from New York to Chicago on the electric cars with only two twenty-mile recourses to (ugh!) steam—between Hoosick Falls and Mechanicsville (via the Boston & Maine) and between Fonda and Little Falls (the New York Central was available). Twenty-five lines, if you were up to it.

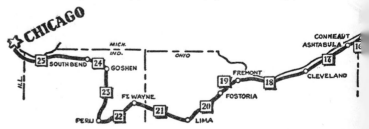

wisely. Glib promoters and prideful local boosters, with little regard for traffic potential, brought many lines into being where scarcely a chance for success existed. Big-city street-railway companies and electric utilities frequently went into the interurban business, and such giant enterprises as the Milwaukee Electric Railway & Light Company provided not only electric power and local streetcar lines but also fast interurban service over large areas. In some parts of the United States, principally in New England and the Far West, steam railroads developed extensive interurban systems that acted as freight and passenger feeder-lines to the parent road.

But far more often steam railroads and the interurbans were bitter rivals, for the electric cars cut heavily into local travel on the steam trains, and sometimes even made a dent in their light-freight and express revenues. Every possible obstacle was usually placed in the way of electric-line construction, and many an interurban, unable to obtain a grade crossing with a steam line, was forced to construct an expensive overpass or underpass. On a few occasions things got rough. Late in 1906, rival construction forces of the Northern Electric Railway and George Gould's Western Pacific, both building toward Sacramento, arrived in Marysville, California, at about the same time. The two routes crossed at a point just south of the Yuba River, where an apiary was located. The Western Pacific men got their rails down first, but the interurban's track gang arrived soon after, and on January 12, 1907, the famous "Battle of the Bee Farm" took place when a hundred Northern Electric men tore out all of the newly laid Western Pacific rails and put down their own. Once the electric cars were running, the steam roads often tried to beat them at their own game, setting up equally frequent schedules at cut-rate fares. Such tactics proved costly and futile, and were usually soon abandoned.

By 1917, when the construction boom had pretty well subsided, there were over 18,000 miles of interurban trackage in the United States and almost 10,000

cars were in operation. Many of the southern, southwestern, and mountain states had only a few miles of track, but few were entirely without any. The interurban achieved its greatest growth in five midwestern states: Ohio, Indiana, Michigan, Illinois, and Wisconsin; more than forty per cent of the nation's interurban mileage was concentrated in them, largely because of the flatness of the landscape, which cut down construction costs. In Ohio and Indiana the traction network reached almost every city and town of any consequence. There was said to be an interurban line wrapped around nearly every Indiana county courthouse. Indianapolis was America's greatest traction center, with hundreds of miles of track radiating outward in a dozen directions. During 1914, seven million passengers arrived in Indianapolis' Traction Terminal; 520 passenger cars and nearly 100 freight cars departed daily.

The greatest of all America's traction systems was the Pacific Electric Railway, which radiated in every direction from Los Angeles with over 1,000 miles of lines, and reached over 125 cities and communities in southern California. Pacific Electric was largely the work of Henry E. Huntington, wealthy nephew of Collis P. Huntington, one of the Southern Pacific's "Big Four," who acquired a pioneer Los Angeles–Pasadena electric line in 1901 and, in little over a decade, built it into a giant.

Many of Pacific Electric's interurban routes were conceived for purposes of real-estate promotion, and Huntington's profits from his Pacific Electric Land Company were probably at least as great as those earned by his electric cars. Much of southern California grew up along Pacific Electric lines, and such now-populous and prominent areas as Hollywood, Beverly Hills, and the San Fernando Valley were little more than open fields until the "big red cars" arrived.

But the grandest, most intriguing interurban scheme of them all was the Chicago–New York Air Line. Its promoters proposed to build a 750-mile, double-track "super railroad" between the two cities that would be fully 160 miles shorter than any steam route, with running times "10 hours quicker than the quickest" and fares "$10 cheaper than the cheapest." Captivated by the enthusiasm of the line's founder and president, Alexander C. Miller, thousands rushed to buy stock.

As the tracks inched across northern Indiana, the stockholders' interest and enthusiasm were bolstered by a monthly newspaper, the *Air Line News*, which trumpeted even the smallest progress as a major achievement, and by such booster organizations as the Kankakee Air Line Stockholders' Association of the World. But Miller's impossibly high construction

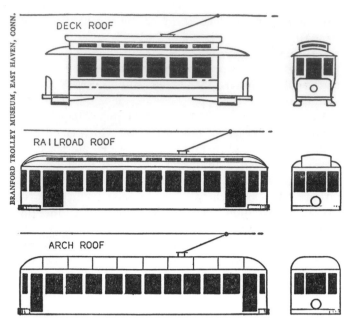

DECK ROOF

RAILROAD ROOF

ARCH ROOF

The evolving design of its cars documents the interurban industry's drive for speed. At first, trolleys with old-fashioned "deck" roofs were used. Larger cars with "railroad" roofs, streamlined at both ends, were in vogue until 1920. Finally came "arch" roofs, rounded at sides and ends.

standards created prohibitive costs, and progress was disappointingly slow. Four years were spent constructing a tremendous fill, nearly two miles long and 180 feet wide at the base, across Coffey Creek Bottoms, east of Gary, Indiana. The mighty mound of earth was finally completed, but it helped empty the Air Line treasury and exhausted the stockholders' patience. With less than thirty miles of its arrow-straight track built, and only one pair of glossy interurban cars (lettered "Chicago" at one end and "New York" at the other) to show for its promoters' efforts, the Air Line wound up as part of just another small system.

Interurban men, as a rule, refrained from the sort of "public be damned" shenanigans practiced by the steam-railroad barons of earlier days. There were occasional lapses, however. In 1924 Valentine Winters, manager of the Dayton & Western Traction Company, became involved in a squabble with the officials of New Lebanon, Ohio, over paving between the rails which traversed city streets. Unable to reach a satisfactory agreement, Winters disdainfully ripped them up and built a new line around New Lebanon on private right of way. "New Lebanon says Winters is bluffing," headlined a Dayton newspaper at the height of the controversy, which may have had something to do with the name "Valley Bluff" which Winters gave the new station just outside town.

Traction lines were normally constructed in the hope of making a profit for the stockholders, but there

were several devoted to more lofty objectives. The Winona Interurban Railway, in Indiana, was constructed by the Winona Assembly and Summer School Session, and its profits went to the operation of a trade school for poor children. When a Tulsa, Oklahoma, oilman established the Sand Springs Home to care for orphans and for widows with children, he endowed it liberally with tracts of industrial land and a multitude of business enterprises, chief among them an interurban, the Sand Springs Railway, which carried passengers until 1954.

Almost from the beginning, interurban proprietors were alert for new methods of attracting extra revenue. Amusement parks were one of the most common traffic builders, and many a company had an "Electric Park" or its equivalent located along its route. When the Stark Electric Railroad was built in northern Ohio soon after the turn of the century, an elaborate park was included in the construction plans. A pond that was dammed to provide water for the line's power-house was also stocked with fish, and a large fleet of rowboats was purchased for rental. Playground equipment and picnic facilities were installed on the edge of the pond, and a dance pavilion was erected. Skating on the pond built up winter traffic on the cars.

Pacific Electric operated the world's largest bath house and salt-water plunge at Redondo Beach, California, and an auto race track, the Motordrome, near Playa del Rey. But its greatest tourist attraction was the famed Mount Lowe line, originally built in 1893 by Professor Thaddeus S. C. Lowe, the Civil War balloonist. Interurban cars carried excursionists from Los Angeles up Rubio Canyon, north of Pasadena, to a hotel, dance hall, and refreshment stand. Above Rubio the Great Cable Incline carried them to the summit of Echo Mountain, and there two additional hotels, the Chalet and Echo Mountain House, were surrounded by such attractions as hiking trails and bridle paths, a zoo, a museum, and an observatory equipped with a sixteen-inch telescope. The three-million-candlepower Great World's Fair Searchlight, which Professor Lowe bought and installed on Echo Mountain in 1894, was visible 150 miles at sea.

Above Echo Mountain a narrow-gauge "Alpine Division" carried the excursionists through spectacular mountain scenery to Mount Lowe Springs, where a fourth hotel, the Alpine Tavern, was built 1,100 feet below the summit of the mountain. The narrow-gauge track wound through 127 curves in four miles, and crossed eighteen trestles, one of which described an almost complete circle. The roadbed was carved out of solid granite throughout its entire length.

Widely advertised as "the Greatest Mountain Trolley Trip in the World," the Mount Lowe line operated for over forty years, but troubles plagued it from the start. Fire destroyed Echo Mountain House in 1900, and in 1905 a windstorm toppled the Chalet and started a fire that destroyed every building on Echo Mountain but the observatory. A landslide smashed Rubio Hotel to the canyon floor in 1909, and in 1936 a fire wiped out the last hotel. Two years later a cloudburst destroyed most of the railway itself.

A number of midwestern interurbans constructed baseball parks to stimulate traffic, and several Ohio lines organized leagues among communities along their lines. The Cleveland & Southwestern Baseball Trolley League included six towns reached by the interurban; the railway donated a silver cup to the winning team, assisted in advertising the games, and offered free rides to the players. One of the line's officials acted as president of the league.

Various kinds of "theatre specials" were always popular on the interurbans. During the twenties the Chicago, North Shore & Milwaukee operated Grand Opera Specials during the opera season and served a light supper on the return trip. As recently as the mid-fifties it still operated special excursion trains to the Chicago Symphony Orchestra's concerts at Ravinia Park, north of Evanston. Nowadays, one inches home hungry through the traffic.

Special trains were often operated for company picnics, lodge outings, and similar excursions of the celluloid-collar set, and almost every interurban line of any consequence maintained one or more ornate parlor cars for charter service. As an early text on the operation of electric railways observed, "The chartered car appeals to the feelings of exclusiveness, sense of ownership and comfort beloved of most humans."

Travel over really great distances never amounted to much, but some rather lengthy interurban trips were possible. One could ride from Shawmut, a little town just north of Waterville, Maine, along a series of connecting lines to New York City and then, after crossing the Hudson River by ferry, continue on as far south as Delaware City, Delaware, or as far west as Newville, Pennsylvania. A 1903 article in *World's Work,* which praised the benefits of the "trolley vacation," outlined a trip from Boston to New York that required two days of "hard and steady electric travel" and cost $3.28 in fares. Trolley travel between the two cities became a little less arduous and expensive a few years later when the Old Colony Street Railway Company joined in an overnight trolley-steamer service. Travellers boarded the cars at Post Office Square in Boston for the trip to Fall River, where they transferred to steamers for the overnight run to New York. The cost of that entire trip, a comfortable one, was only $1.75. (Present cost, by railroad, one way, is $11.58; by air, $16, not counting travel to airports; in turnpike tolls alone, $3.30.)

In 1915 the *Interurban Trolley Guide* outlined for the "enthusiastic trolley tourist" a Chicago-to-New York trip which could then be made entirely on interurban lines with the exception of two short stretches in New York State, where it was necessary to use steam trains. The journey took anywhere from thirty-one to forty-five hours, depending on connections, cost about twenty-one dollars, and covered twenty-five different electric railways. Needless to say, the arrangement never caused undue concern on the part of competing steam-railway officials.

One of the first efforts by the trolley people to invade the steam roads' long-haul, luxury market came in 1905, when three electric lines joined in the operation of the deluxe Interstate Limited between Indianapolis and Dayton. The special cars were luxuriously appointed, and a buffet between the two usual compartments—the smoker and the "ladies' parlor"—served light meals from a menu said to be every bit the equal of those on Pullman buffet cars.

Sleeping-car service was soon afterward commenced by the Illinois Traction lines, on the 172-mile main line from St. Louis to Peoria. In a time before air-conditioning, cinder-free sleepers had distinct advantages over steam-railroad Pullmans. Illinois Traction's berths were fully six inches longer, and its cars were twenty years ahead of Pullman's in providing windows for upper-berth passengers. Every berth had a plush-lined safe-deposit box, and porters served free coffee and rolls in the morning. Only two other lines ever followed Illinois Traction's lead.

Speed was always a matter of concern with electric-railway men. Even though many interurban cars were capable of whisking along at well over sixty miles per hour, over-all running times were anything but rapid during the early years, for tracks were rarely up to it and almost every line had to pass through the streets of cities and towns. As late as 1906 three Ohio interurbans were claiming the "fastest electric service in the world," but even their "limiteds" averaged only about thirty-two miles per hour. In local service, they could easily outpace their steam competitors, but when the interurbans made their bid for the long-haul trade, they were at first at a disadvantage.

Many lines stood by conventional car designs, and produced big, powerful steel cars capable of very high speeds. On his three Chicago interurbans, the midwestern utilities magnate Samuel Insull not only introduced handsome new steel cars but spent millions reconstructing and relocating tracks. "Did you ever travel 80 miles an hour?" challenged North Shore Line ads, and all the Insull interurbans enjoyed their most profitable years during the 1920's.

Unlike Insull, many traction operators could not afford to reconstruct their roadbeds, and the quest for speed therefore concentrated on new designs for a fast, light car that could operate smoothly over rough track. In 1929 Dr. Thomas Conway, Jr., led a group of investors who assembled the Cincinnati & Lake Erie Railroad from several failing properties, and immediately ordered twenty radical, high-speed interurban cars in an effort to win back the system's declining traffic. They made wide use of aluminum and were equipped with the most powerful motors ever installed in cars of comparable size and weight. They were capable of speeds in excess of ninety miles per hour; in the extensive publicity that surrounded their introduction in 1930, one of them was raced against—and ostensibly defeated—an airplane.

The same year Dr. Conway acquired control of another interurban, the Philadelphia & Western, which was also badly in need of new equipment. The Conway management, setting out to construct an even better car than their Cincinnati & Lake Erie lightweight, launched an intensive research program. In a wind tunnel at the University of Michigan, Professor Felix W. Pawlowski determined that a streamlined car body could be constructed which at speeds over sixty miles per hour would save forty per cent or more of the energy required to move conventional equipment. The ten all-aluminum Bullet cars which were the result of this study could make ninety-two miles per hour.

Almost every interurban was built with an eye toward the passenger trade, but most of them found freight traffic a profitable sideline. Steep grades and the sharp curves common in city streets ruled out the use of standard freight cars on many of the lines, and the interurbans designed and built their own cars for hauling light freight. The service was fast, especially by modern standards, and Indiana interurban people boasted that they could deliver shipments anywhere within seventy-five miles of Indianapolis on the same day the goods were ordered. In 1902 interurban lines took in about two million dollars for hauling such commodities as newspapers, mail, milk, and express. By 1922, their freight operations were bringing in forty-five million dollars a year. Interurbans were "piggybacking" truck trailers on flatcars years before the steam railroads enthusiastically adopted the idea. Insull's North Shore Line was the pioneer, in 1926.

No one realized it at the time, of course, but the interurban was doomed almost from the beginning. The villain was the automobile, which had already been invented before the interurban's heyday. Few traction men took it seriously at first; and a few interurbans

even found a source of extra revenue in the automobile. In 1905 the general superintendent of the Lake Shore Electric Railway, noting the frequency with which farmers were hauling in disabled cars from the highway that paralleled the railway all the way from Cleveland to Toledo, established an "automobile am-

A familiar cartoon commentary on rural electric-line travel was Fontaine Fox's "Toonerville Trolley," begun in 1908. At the end, alas, Fox's wonderful trolley gave way to a bus.

bulance" service. It employed a specially equipped flatcar drawn by a freight locomotive. The service, which cost fifteen dollars and up, was said to be "much less embarrassing than having to resort to the horse to get back to town." For a few years around the end of the twenties the Pacific Northwest Traction Company did a lively business hauling trucks, buses, and automobiles around gaps in the uncompleted Pacific Highway north of Seattle.

But gradually the auto began to win out. A few of the weaker interurbans failed soon after World War I, and by the end of the twenties the whole traction network was beginning to crumble as hard-surfaced highways and mass-produced cars spread across the land. Bold, depression-induced interurban consolidations such as the Indiana Railroad System and Ohio's Cincinnati & Lake Erie served only to delay the inevitable; both were gone by World War II. A few lines survived into the war years and enjoyed a brief revival of the bonanza traffic they had once known. Henry

Huntington's vast Pacific Electric network, for example, which went into the war virtually intact, handled more passengers in 1945 (109 million of them) than at any other time in its history. But by 1961 the last of its many passenger routes had switched to buses.

The earliest interurban of all, the Portland–Oregon City line, came close to being the last; it survived until early in 1958, having served the Willamette Valley for sixty-five years. Samuel Insull's Chicago lines had become commuter carriers of major importance, but once the wartime traffic had ceased and new roads and freeways made commuting by private automobile as fast as taking the interurbans, the Chicago, Aurora & Elgin and the North Shore line folded up. Of the three Insull interurbans, only the South Shore line continues in operation. The line loses over $500,000 a year on its passenger business, but freight-hauling is so profitable that it offsets the loss. Now major railroads are making efforts to buy control of the South Shore, and once this is accomplished, there will almost certainly be attempts to cut down, and then eliminate, passenger service; the road will probably end up as a dieselized branch of a larger railroad line.

The only other commercial interurban line in Canada or the United States is operated between Upper Darby and Norristown, Pennsylvania, by the Philadelphia Suburban Transportation Company. Recently it purchased two high-speed, streamlined, four-section articulated interurban trains from the defunct Chicago North Shore line and placed them in rush-hour service to supplement Dr. Conway's wind-tunnel-designed Bullet cars, which are now showing their age. The new trains contain a vanishing amenity, a bar-lounge section for suburban commuters. How long this service will last is problematical, especially in view of the impending takeover of the line by a transit authority. Authorities and amenities rarely go together.

The interurban may be nearly gone, but it will not soon be forgotten. Once it was evident that the few remaining lines were disappearing and their cars and other equipment were headed for the scrap heap, a new fraternity arose—trolley-museum enthusiasts, who now number in the thousands. Several museum groups have been formed for the sole purpose of saving representative interurban cars by purchasing them at scrap prices, buying an abandoned right of way, and putting the cars in service again for the entertainment of children who have never ridden an interurban and of their elders in whom nostalgia runs strong.

A dozen such lines are now in service, and more are in the planning stage. The largest, and the first to be formed, is located at Kennebunkport, Maine, where the right of way of a defunct interurban line was purchased all the way to Biddeford, six miles to the north.

Although only a mile of track is now in operation, more than eighty trolleys and interurban cars have been acquired, and the line, the Seashore Electric Railway, can eventually build its track right into the streets of Biddeford. Similar lines run at Branford and Warehouse Point, Connecticut, with cars of many varieties.

The real interurban is gone—yet not quite. The highways and freeways that doomed so many interurban lines—simply because it was much cheaper to run a bus over someone else's roads than to build a railroad with expensive poles and overhead wire—are now so overburdened that in rush hours traffic stagnates. The answer in all urban areas now is clearly rapid transit, the electrically operated rail line that can whisk riders into and out of cities without the long rush-hour delays.

Consider, for instance, Louisville, Kentucky, where sixty-five years ago a rapid-transit system was developed at considerable cost. It took riders from suburban areas into downtown Louisville along seven different routes by interurban lines of the Louisville & Interurban Railroad. Then the automobile and bus came along, and the competition was too much. The interurban lines gave up and were dismantled. The rights of way were sold. Today city planners in Louisville, as in San Francisco, Washington, and most other swollen urban complexes, are planning vast expenditures for rapid-transit lines. What routes will they take? You guessed it: much the same as the interurbans of the past. As Louisville's city works director says, "I think we're coming around full-cycle on this thing. It's a shame that the old interurban lines didn't survive."

The big old electric car, dusting through the meadows with its air horn shrieking for the crossings, is only a museum piece. Yet something is coming back, something without the wicker and the inlaid woodwork, something a little too streamlined and shiny perhaps, but something to hearten those who loved the most open road of all, the rails of the interurban.

William D. Middleton is the author of The Interurban Era *and the forthcoming* Time of the Trolley. *A lieutenant commander in the Navy's Civil Engineer Corps, he is currently on active duty in Da Nang, Viet Nam, whence he writes us: "I always make a practice of looking into railway operations wherever I am, and you might be interested to know that the old French-built, meter-gauge Saigon–Hanoi railway is now in operation from Da Nang north through Hué to a point just short of the 17th parallel. A daily round trip is operated (when the train doesn't get blown up) behind a steam locomotive, which pushes along a tanklike armored car in front of it." Once a rail buff, always a rail buff.*

Last Ghastly Moments at the Little Bighorn

CONTINUED FROM PAGE 21

horses run right into each other—the horses both fell down and rolled, and he nearly ran into them himself, but managed to turn aside. The dust was so thick he could hardly see. He swung his horse out and turned to charge back in again, close to the end of the fight, and suddenly the dust lifted away. He saw a troop flag [guidon] not far in front of him. Over on the other side some soldiers were still fighting, so he galloped past and picked the flag up and rode into the fight, and he used it to count coup on a soldier.

After the suicide boys came in, it did not take long: half an hour perhaps. Many have agreed with what Wolftooth said, that if it had not been for the suicide boys, it might have ended the way it did at the Reno fight. The Indians all stayed back and fought there; no suicide boys jumped in to begin the hand-to-hand fight. The Custer fight was different because these boys went in that way, and it was their rule to be killed.

Another thing many of the Northern Cheyennes said was that if Custer had kept going—if he had not waited there on the ridge so long—he could have made it back to Reno. But he probably thought he could stand off the Indians and win.

Everyone always wanted to know who killed Custer. I have interpreted twice for people asking about this, and whether anyone ever saw a certain Indian take a shot and kill him. But all the Indians say too many people were shooting; nobody could tell whose bullet killed a certain man. There were rumors some knew but would not say anything for fear of trouble. But it was more like Spotted Blackbird said: "If we could have seen where each bullet landed, we might have known. But hundreds of bullets were flying that day."

After the Indians had killed every soldier, my grandmother's brother, Tall Bull, came across the river and said, "Get a travois fixed. One of the dead is my

CULVER PICTURES

brother-in-law, and we will have to go over and get his body." It was my grandfather, Lame White Man. So they went across to where he was lying. He did not have his war clothes on; as I said, he had not had time. And some Sioux had made a mistake on him. They thought he was an Indian scout with Custer—they often fought undressed that way. And his scalp was gone from the top of his head. Nearby was the body of another Cheyenne, one of the suicide boys.

I heard the Sioux lost sixty-six men and the Northern Cheyennes just seven, but there might have been more. The Indian dead were all moved from the battlefield right away.

Many Indians were up on the battlefield after it was over, getting the dead or taking things from the soldiers. I asked Grandmother if she went. Women were up there as well as men. But she said the fight was still going on up above with Reno, and many women were afraid to go near the field. They thought the soldiers might break away and come in their direction.

White Wolf (also called Shot in the Head), who was in this fight, said that afterwards a lot of young men searched the soldiers' pockets. That square green paper money was in them, so they took some. Later when they were making mud horses, they used the money for saddle blankets. Silver money was found too. The Northern Cheyennes made buckles out of it.

The camp broke up the next day after the battle. Some people even left that evening to move up near Lodge Grass. Some of the warriors stayed behind to go on fighting with Reno, but they did not stay more than a day. They knew other soldiers were in the country, and they were out of meat and firewood. They split into many groups, some following the river, and others going up Reno Creek and to other places.

By the time the other soldiers [Terry's men] got to the battlefield, the Indians were gone. A Cheyenne named Lost Leg rode back a few days later looking for horses. A lot had strayed away and he thought he might be able to get some of them. He said he could smell the battlefield a long way off. He had planned to go in and look at it, but he could not even come close, it was so strong. So he gave up and returned.

There was no more real fighting that summer.

Margot Liberty has lived with the Northern Cheyennes and spent a year as a historian, interpreter, and guide for the National Park Service at the Custer Battlefield Monument. She now teaches anthropology at the University of Minnesota. She and Mr. Stands in Timber have worked together on a history of the Northern Cheyennes soon to be published by the Yale University Press.

THE GRISLY EPILOGUE

A new book by the eminent western historian and AMERI-CAN HERITAGE contributor Mari Sandoz may prove to be the definitive account of Custer's defeat. The Battle of the Little Bighorn, to be published in May by J. B. Lippincott, relates in scrupulous detail the events that led up to the battle, the hand-to-hand fighting in which Custer died, and the subsequent struggle between the Indians and the remnants of Custer's command under Reno and Benteen. Finally, in a chapter from which the following excerpt is taken, Miss Sandoz describes the frightful scene that greeted the troops of General Alfred Terry and Colonel John Gibbon as they arrived two days later upon the silent field.

At reveille [on June] twenty-seventh not an enemy was in sight anywhere. The column [Terry's infantry] started out early, marching along the evener bench west of the river valley while Lieutenant Bradley and his mounted men [part of Terry's command] scouted the breaks and ridges along the right side of the stream. From a highish point they noticed strange objects scattered over the hills rising far ahead—buffaloes, probably an Indian hunt, the whitish carcasses skinned to the tallow, the dark not yet touched. But curiously there was no movement, no butchering women and children running from one animal to the next, no men packing the meat on horses, no one standing guard.

Terry halted when the glasses showed the first signs of the deserted Indian camp—the Cheyenne village, the ribs of the wickiups and bare gaunt lodge poles like curious clumps of weed sticks in the hot sun. There were more dusky patches farther on—as though a great Indian encampment had stretched in scattered villages up along the river for miles. But not one twist of smoke rose in the air, nothing that could be identified as a movement anywhere, except an eagle flying, or buzzards dropping to the far ridge where it seemed there had been the buffalo hunt.

The horse droppings, the freshly worn pony trails to water from the upland prairie, were beyond anything Terry or Gibbon had ever seen—speaking of great herds, many, many thousands of animals. Through all this sign of an overwhelming force the column was kept moving in uneasiness, the old campaigners certain they were being watched by hidden Sioux scouts, with no telling how many of the warriors of this great camp might be waiting in ambush.

The bearded Terry slumped in the saddle, his eyes alert, his dusty face sweat-streaked in the early morning heat of the sun, the regimental colors sagging in the stillness of the air. On the ridge across the river a mile or more away Bradley and his men were riding among the dark objects, going from one to the other, but apparently without haste, even dismounting.

Then Bradley, pale under the dust and sunshine, and silent, plunged through the flooded stream and hurried to Terry. Saluting with parade-ground formality, he approached to report that they had examined the strange-looking objects along the hills to the east—197 dead men

of Custer's force, stripped to the bloated, discoloring skin, most of them unrecognizable, the dark objects their horses, all dead for two, three days.

Early in the morning of the twenty-eighth, Reno ordered Captain McDougall and his Troop B to the Indian camps to search out implements to bury the dead. With what he could scare up—very little—the captain crossed the river in the bright morning sun. Spreading his force out in a sad skirmish line, he moved up from the river, searching through hollows and clumps of sagebrush. They found them, most of the men dead in the ravine. From a distance it was plain they had used the upper sides of the cut bank as a sort of breastwork, sliding down as they were struck. Bloated and blackened as the naked bodies were, the faces like the wounds, puffed and swollen, oozing and flyblown, few were recognizable. The captain had a record kept of those who could be identified, pathetically few, although he had known many of the troopers for years. One definite identification was a sergeant because he had one sock on, with his name still plain.

But in the heat and stench the men trying to examine the decomposing bodies began to vomit so violently that McDougall finally had great chunks of earth and sod cut from the banks of the wide draw and thrown down upon the dead of Company E, covering them as well as possible, filling in much of the ravine's depth for all time, changing and obliterating much of the site.

Elsewhere other burial details moved over the ground. The bodies were all in similar condition on this third day of heat. Most of the dead were completely naked, many scalped and hacked, although it was no longer always possible to distinguish the wounds of actual combat from later mutilations. Custer's stripped body had been found in a sort of sitting position between two troopers in the low pile of dead behind the breastwork that was a tangle of stiff horse legs sticking out.

The body of Tom Custer [Custer's brother] was face down, most of his scalp gone except some tufts of hair at the nape. The skull was crushed, with several arrows shot into it and into his back. The features, which had been pressed into the ground, were flattened and decomposed, unrecognizable, but on one arm, broken by a shot, were the tattooed initials TWC with the goddess of liberty and the flag.

Altogether, the soldiers buried 212 bodies, bringing the dead, with the missing and Reno's losses, to 265, including sixteen officers, seven civilians, and three Indian scouts. Without proper tools to dig the hard-baked and gravelly earth of the Custer ridge, the bodies were not buried in the usual deep graves or trenches. They were covered, but so thinly that those who knew the swift gully-washers and cloudbursts of the dry country realized that some of the bodies would surely be washed out before fall, or covered by fill-ins beyond all finding, many of the poor markers set up at the graves of the officers certain to be swept away.

"Lady" Knox CONTINUED FROM PAGE 47

perhaps there was an unconscious reason for her fixation—he was tall, built like a heavyweight prize fighter; Lucy herself was plump, her pretty face poised upon a hefty body. Here was a man who could make her feel petite and fragile.

At last the Fluckers gave in, and the wedding took place on June 16, 1774, shortly before Lucy's eighteenth birthday and Harry's twenty-fifth. The Fluckers tried to make their unwelcome son-in-law respectable by offering him a commission in the British Army. He was promising material, being a well-trained officer of the militia and a self-taught student of military history and tactics. Harry politely refused and went on studying his military books for other purposes. He was supported in his decision by Lucy. The parents groaned and pointed out that Lucy's older sister, Hannah, had married a fine British officer, and her brother Thomas was also in the King's service. Obviously, they said, Lucy and her rebellious bookseller were bound to end up "eating the bread of poverty and dependence."

In April, 1775, came bloodshed at Lexington and Concord, and Harry made up his mind. The decision to offer the fruit of his military studies to the cause of liberty was inevitable for him, but for Lucy it was a drastic break with her family and past life. There is no record to show that Henry Knox was with the American forces until late in June, so there may have been a period of doubt as to what she ought to do. But it ended unequivocally, and they took flight to Cambridge together.

Henry Knox was one of the few volunteers who had any idea of military engineering or the use of artillery. He was immediately put to work designing and building defensive forts at Roxbury, while Lucy, left among other Army wives in Worcester, spent her time awaiting letters and writing them. She poured out her soul to "my ever dear Harry," together with complaints and domestic detail. She was filled with pride that her Harry was indispensable, but sobbed with self-pity at their separation. She rejoiced that General George Washington, on his arrival at Cambridge, praised Harry's defense works at Roxbury and, following John Adams' advice to make good use of the young student of military tactics, appointed him commander of artillery. Harry suggested to the new Commander in Chief that an expedition be made to Fort Ticonderoga to fetch the equipment captured from the British by Ethan Allen. Thus Lucy had a glimpse of her Harry in November, as he travelled through Worcester to start the mission, and again in January, when he returned with fifty-nine precious pieces of artillery that had been brought through snow and ice. These same guns, dragged onto Dorchester Heights above Boston, were trained upon the city and caused the flight of Lucy's parents in the general evacuation by the British and their Tory sympathizers. (See "Big Guns for Washington" in the April, 1955, AMERICAN HERITAGE.)

Throughout the next two years, Lucy's life consisted of snatched visits with Harry alternated with dreary months in strange houses. She dashed to Harry's side when Boston fell, and managed to go along with him when he toured New England ports to plan for their defense. She had to be left behind in Fairfield, Connecticut, for the birth of their first child, Lucy Flucker Knox, while Harry joined General Washington in New York. But she was soon with him again, in spite of warnings that the unpredictable General Howe might attack the city at any time. She was delighted with the house, at No. 1 Broadway, requisitioned for Knox's headquarters, and she basked in the deference shown to her splendidly military husband, now a colonel, commander in chief of artillery, and on intimate terms with General Washington. In July the Knoxes joyfully celebrated the reading of the Declaration of Independence, but hardly had time to savor the heady moment, for suddenly the British fleet loomed off Staten Island.

Harry sent Lucy back to Fairfield, where she slumped in misery. All the news was bad; there was a rout on Long Island, New York City was taken, the Continental Army had retreated into New Jersey. A family Christmas with their first-born was impossible; Harry was on the banks of the Delaware using his mighty voice to shout General Washington's orders to each unit as it embarked across the stormy river. He wrote to Lucy of the successful crossing, the triumph at Trenton, action at Princeton, the pause at Morristown. Lucy pleaded to join him, hotly denying that she had ever complained or needed luxury: "I was pleased with the inconvenience" (did Harry raise a humorous eyebrow?)—"nothing but bread and water might I be within twenty miles of you." She learned that Mrs. Washington and Mrs. Horatio Gates had been with their husbands. "Happy Mrs. Gates, Happy Mrs. Washington—in the last ten months we have not spent six weeks together."

Harry wrote whenever he could, though constantly at General Washington's side and occupied with a thousand duties concerning supervision of artillery and training of recruits. "Nothing but the call of a country much injured and misunderstood to whom I am inseparably connected," he wrote, "would have called me from the arms and company of her who is inexpressibly interwoven with my heart."

Lucy had shown the force of her passions when she fought her parents for permission to marry, and tantrums had succeeded in the defeat of Papa and Mamma. Now she was faced with life in a historic moment which could not be changed to suit her, and with a husband who recognized its solemnity and put his duty first. And there were no longer parents to comfort her. Perhaps when she fled from Boston it had been rather fun to defy them, but now she felt deep hurt that no letter came from them. Through an aunt she learned that Mr. Flucker continued to draw a salary of £300 as Provincial Secretary and worked to obtain compensation for dispossessed Tories, savagely denying the claims of those he suspected had ever shown the least sympathy for the American cause, as if hitting out at his daughter through them.

Harry was never spared a detail of her anxieties and loneliness. At Fairfield she complained of the company as "unrefined as yeomanry," and earned a lecture on democracy from Harry. From Wallingford, Connecticut, where she and a Mrs. Pollard rented a house together, their landlord wrote to Colonel Knox to report the crockery broken and the cellar of West Indian rum consumed, and without actually accusing the ladies he may have given Harry fears that his young wife was drowning her sorrows. It was a relief when Lucy moved back to Boston, where she had friends and could also be kept busy helping Harry's brother Billy run the bookstore.

When the Continental Army encamped at Valley Forge for the winter of 1777, Lucy was at last allowed to join her husband. She bloomed in contentment in a big stone house beside Harry's artillery park and became a pleasing hostess to cold and threadbare officers. Somehow the Knoxes always managed to provide extra food and wine, and at night there was often dancing and singing. At this time the relationship between the Washingtons and the Knoxes burgeoned. Henry Knox was already as close to the Commander in Chief as any officer in Washington's working "family," but now the ladies became close in spite of twenty-five years' difference in age. Both came from a background of privilege, Martha's accomplishments being those of a country lady, while Lucy's were more urban and official. Lucy grew in self-importance as she informed the older woman on matters of protocol. Together the Knoxes were of special value to the Washingtons in this moment of open criticism of the General. Never a word of criticism was spoken by Henry and Lucy Knox.

With spring came the glorious news that France had recognized the American republic and would send aid. A Maytime Thanksgiving was celebrated. Then camp was broken, the men prepared for battle, and the women scattered to their homes. The separation of soldiers and wives was brief this summer, however, for by August the last major battle in the North was fought at Monmouth and the army settled down to await a move by the British in New York. The new encampment was at Pluckemin, New Jersey, where Harry created an artillery park with an "academy" attached for the training of officers (the forerunner of West Point). Lucy joined him, and there enjoyed an almost settled life for nearly two years. The Knoxes gave a ball on February 18, 1779, attended by seventy ladies and three hundred gentlemen. It was opened by General Washington, who led Lucy onto the floor for a minuet (in spite of her advanced pregnancy). There was dinner, a fireworks display, and dancing till dawn. General Washington accepted the challenge of Kitty Greene, General Nathanael Greene's giddy wife, and danced for three uninterrupted hours.

Massive French help and plans for a concerted attack put an end to life at Pluckemin. Harry hurried away to collect the largest supply of artillery he could raise and see it transported to Yorktown, while Lucy went to Mount Vernon, where she became a pleasant but somewhat managing companion to Martha Washington. The visit was marred for Lucy by envy of the fine house and established living of the Virginia plantation, and she wrote Harry of her longings for a home of their own. He had little time to give the matter thought: the American-French forces were besieging Yorktown for two weeks and finally, on October 19, 1781, achieved the surrender of General Cornwallis. For his contribution Henry Knox was made a major general—the youngest in the American forces.

The Knoxes lived through the prolonged period of near-peace at Newburgh, New York. Harry was in command at West Point and had the melancholy duty of disbanding the Army, to whom years of back pay were still owed. After peace was signed, Harry and Lucy moved to a house at Dorchester, outside Boston (later Daniel Webster's summer home), and then to a house on Boston Common rented from the painter John Singleton Copley. Lucy's pregnancies had been following fast upon each other— a son named for General Henry Jackson; a little boy who died; another boy, Marcus; and a girl, Julia Wadsworth. The Flucker estates were now Lucy's, awarded to her as the only non-Tory member of the Flucker family; Harry, administrator for his wife, looked over the Maine lands

while on a mission to the Penobscot Indians. Speculation in undeveloped territory was the rage, and Harry enthusiastically bought up the patents of other heirs. He noted the fine sweep of the St. Georges River as seen from the settlement at Thomaston, and deemed it an ideal spot for a future home for Lucy. It had to remain a dream for the moment, however, because the Confederation made Henry Knox "Secretary at War," in charge of both Army and Navy.

In March, 1785, Henry Knox took up his new duties in New York at a salary of $2,450, considerably less than his household expenses. There was little to do at first because there was neither an army nor a navy, but he busied himself drawing up plans for an effective defense force. Lucy, annoyed that Harry had rented a country house on Bowery Lane ("I am an urban person"), arrived from Boston in June with the children. The house was four miles out from the center of the city, but this did not prevent a continual stream of carriages from arriving to receive the Knox hospitality. Lucy soon got her way, and a fine town house at No. 4 Broadway rang with the voices of her children and was kept lit far into the small hours to the sound of music, laughter, and the cries of Lucy's victims at whist. Harry anxiously made a breakdown of yearly costs, calculated in pounds: total expenditures £1,304; salary, £980; discrepancy, £324, to be met by borrowing on Lucy's estates. Their extravagant living became fashionable gossip. Lucy had added to the mouths to feed by producing four more children in less than four years: William Bingham, Caroline (who lived less than a year), Augusta, and George Washington.

New York became livelier still as the national capital under the Presidency of George Washington. The "Secretary at War" became Secretary of War. He was one of the most experienced department heads, and his position was further enhanced by his friendship of fourteen years with the President. It was the Knoxes who were called upon to shop for the brown broadcloth of American make for George Washington's inauguration suit, to which they added some handsome buttons with an eagle design. Henry Knox stood close behind the President as he took his oath of office at Federal Hall, and at the end of the crowded day it was to the Knoxes' house that the President came to watch the fireworks display in New York Harbor.

Their impressive position seemed expressed in their outward appearance. Harry and Lucy had both become enormously fat. The sturdy youth had turned, at near forty, into a monumental man of 290 pounds, yet easy of step, quick in gesture, erect and alert, with keen gray eyes, his hair powdered and held back in a queue, his left hand always elegantly draped in a black silk handkerchief to conceal the loss of two fingers shot off in a hunting accident. Lucy, now thirty-three, weighed 250 pounds and carried herself with tremendous hauteur. "Her size is enormous," wrote Mrs. William Smith to her mother, Abigail Adams, wife of the Vice President; "I am frightened when I look at her; I verily believe that her waist is as large as three of yours at least." Her clothes made her even more noticeable, flamboyant creations hung about with fichus, bows, cascades of lace, mantillas. She retained a French hairdresser at twenty shillings a month to create some startling edifices upon her head: for instance, a wire skeleton towering a foot high, over which her hair was drawn up to a pinnacle and held by a vast crooked comb from which streamers of black gauze floated down her back. The front hair was puffed out, while the back was finished in something like a man's queue—"she seems to mimic the military style, very disgusting in a female," remarked one observer.

Lucy placed herself firmly in the center of all official activity, certain that she was one of the few who knew how to handle it. Thomas Jefferson, while in Paris as United States minister, recorded in his diary a gossipy report that at a presidential ball in New York, Lucy Knox had pushed herself closely behind President and Mrs. Washington and tried to mount the dais to sit upon the sofa with them—"but unfortunately the wicked sofa was too short." Martha Washington was not present at the ball in question, and the gossip was untrue, but Lucy's grandiose manners laid her open to unkind stories and made her repugnant to those who feared that the new American nation might swing away from its democratic principles. Henry Knox, though never bigoted, was a Federalist. His wife, more a social being than a political one, felt comfortable only in the world of privilege, and it was upon her head that the blame fell from Antifederalists when it was seen that Knox would always align himself with Hamilton against Jefferson—"the shadow of Hamilton," Jefferson called him. The Society of the Cincinnati, founded by Knox for officers of the Revolution, was held up as proof of his aristocratic leanings, particularly because it was a hereditary body in which membership passed to sons.

Henry Knox had not needed Lucy to prod him into large-scale living. It had attracted him as a bookseller in Boston when he made his shop an "elegant morning lounge" and married a girl from the gentry. He believed in his own worth and became a grand seigneur by choice and effort. Still, he was a passionate patriot and swore by the ideals on which the new republic was founded. "I believe a republican government formed upon natural principles . . . may exist a great length of time," he wrote to General Samuel Parsons. "I confess I hate the office of king. It is impossible to restrain their power."

In 1790 the national capital was shifted to Philadelphia, and once more the unwieldy Knox household of children, servants, and household goods had to be moved to another rented house. The John Adamses lent their house, Bush Hill, to the Knoxes until another was ready. In Philadelphia, the President held a Tuesday levee and Mrs. Washington a Friday drawing room. There were more balls, more theatres, and more elegant women than in New York. Lucy became an intimate of the beautiful social leader Anne Bingham, who helped her run up more bills for dazzling clothes and filled her head with dazzling descriptions of life in the great French châteaux. Henry Knox, observing that more money was required to keep his family afloat, joined in financial ventures with Anne's husband, William Bingham, and later was forced to borrow from him. Harry's speculations were usually overly optimistic and seldom successful.

It now looked as if Knox's best hope for solvency lay in the development of his wife's estates. He and Lucy decided that the time had come at last to build the house they had always wanted; and at Thomaston, Maine, a great mansion, which eventually cost $50,000, began to rise upon the river bank. People were shocked at the grandiose scale—did the Knoxes really need twenty-four fireplaces?—but Harry said he wanted a worthy house for Lucy after so many nomadic years. "Mrs. Knox wants a cabin," he said; it was he who demanded a mansion. Knox left Philadelphia at a moment when Washington urgently needed him to help suppress the Whiskey Rebellion, and allowed the responsibility and glory to pass to Hamilton and Anthony Wayne. His thoughts were now exclusively for his family, and he wrote Lucy on his trip down East of "the genuine and unspeakable love of my heart, a love which increases with years and shall never die."

The house on the St. Georges River was ready for the family in June, 1795. The General, Lucy, six children, and assorted servants arrived from Boston on a sloop commanded by Captain Andrew Malcolm of Warren. They sailed into the broad mouth of the river, rounded a bend, and there beheld the big white mansion against a background of spruce, maple, and beech. It was all Lucy had dreamed it would be, a combination of a French château as described by Anne Bingham and a fine Virginia mansion—foreign to the New England landscape. Lucy gave it the fittingly elegant French name of Montpelier. It stood three stories high, topped by a cupola, surrounded by broad piazzas, fronted by columns. A princely house, it was served from a crescent of nine outbuildings behind it—a cookhouse, a distillery, a buttery, an icehouse, stables, blacksmith and carpenter shops, and dwellings for servants, grooms, and gardeners.

Montpelier was flung open to the entire neighborhood for a Fourth of July celebration. There was music and trestle tables piled high with food (it was said an ox and twenty sheep were slaughtered). No one forgot the queenly presence of Lucy—for many it was their only glimpse of her during nearly thirty years of her residence in Maine. No one forgot the first sight of the General, soon a familiar figure in his black clothes, a cane swinging dangerously as he pointed out spots for ornamental gardens, orchards, and grazing pastures. This first party over, another was given for the entire Tarrateen tribe of Indians, who set up wigwams on the lawn. The Indians found it all so delightful that the sojourn stretched into weeks, until Lucy's patience gave out. The General called upon the chiefs and said firmly, "Now that we have had a good visit, you had better go home."

More to Lucy's taste was the visit of the roving Duc de La Rochefoucauld-Liancourt, who later wrote in his *Travels in North America*, "Mrs. Knox is a lady of whom you conceive a still higher opinion the longer you are acquainted with her. Seeing her in Philadelphia, you think of her only as a fortunate player of whist. In her house in the country, you discover she possesses sprightliness, knowledge, a good heart, and an excellent understanding." Then came a big, jolly party consisting of the Binghams, two Bingham children, Anne's sister Miss Willing, the Vicomte de

... oh Harry my dearest friend. you know not—you cannot know how dear you are to me—had I never been parted from you it would have remained a secret to myself—but why do I repent what I have so often told you—can I flatter me. that the language of love will be pleasing, amid the bustle...

Lucy's wifely letters (one is excerpted above) all proved violently that absence makes the heart fonder.

Gleason's Pictorial, 1857

Montpelier, the house Henry Knox built for Lucy at Thomaston, Maine, was like nothing ever before seen "down East."

Noailles, Alexander Baring (later Lord Ashburton), and a Mr. Richards from England. They played cards and billiards, used the stable of saddle horses, and drove in the numerous carriages and smart brakes which, in bad weather, could be brought into quarters below the house to allow passengers to keep dry. And they picnicked along the wooded river banks.

Munificent entertainment at Montpelier became a local legend. Any passing notable was made welcome, or any itinerant preacher. Henry Knox's generosity was acknowledged far and wide; he built a church (with a bell by Paul Revere), a school, and a courthouse. He set up new villages for workers, gave employment to the whole district, and amicably settled squatters' claims.

However, the scattered residents of Thomaston, some 800 souls who worked the land, fished, and traded, found Lucy unwilling to mix with the country folk. She drove out in her carriage reportedly spattering mud on pedestrians without acknowledging their presence; she called on no one and is supposed to have preferred to stand in a slushy road rather than enter a farmhouse while repairs were made on her carriage.

Harry could usually accept Lucy's foibles with hu-

mor and he adored her always. She could babble foolishly and annoy him—as she undoubtedly had in 1783 when she greeted the great news of the Peace of Paris with a complaint about having to find a new home—"This plaguey peace has set us all moving again." One time when she suddenly changed her mind about going riding, Harry told the groom, "John, put Mrs. Knox's horse in the stable and do not take it out again until God Almighty or Mrs. Knox tells you to." Always his anger was softened by compassion. Her extreme behavior at Montpelier may have been caused by the relentless succession of tragedies that did not cease even when the haven in the country was reached. Here William Bingham Knox, aged eleven, and Augusta, aged nine, died on the same day, probably of diphtheria, and within a year, Julia Wasdworth, an enchanting girl of fifteen, died of rapid consumption. Lucy's final pregnancy brought her a stillborn child. A bedroom in Montpelier became known as the "dead room," where each victim in turn was laid out. In the end only three children were spared her of the thirteen she bore—the eldest, Lucy; Henry Jackson, who caused endless heartache by his instability; and the youngest girl, Caroline.

When thoughts of bereavements could be pushed aside, the Knoxes' life for the next ten years was a happy one. They spent winters in Boston and returned to Montpelier in the spring, when Harry toured his acres, planning, expanding, running up debts. Eventually it was Lucy who urged that the Boston winters should be abandoned. It seemed a wise plan, for bills were always soaring and Harry's good humor became ruffled when creditors clamored at the great gates of Montpelier. All his land speculation would pay off in time, he was sure . . .

But suddenly time was no longer his. He swallowed a sharp chicken bone, which lodged in his esophagus, and within three days, on October 25, 1806, he was dead at the age of fifty-six. Life without Harry—eighteen years of it—faced Lucy. When the military funeral was over and the last reverberations of the gun salute were stilled and the rich tones of the Paul Revere bell at Harry's church had dwindled to silence, the frightened birds settled back in the trees and Lucy closed herself into Montpelier.

Her two surviving daughters remained faithfully close. Lucy lived nearby with her husband, a lawyer who assisted his mother-in-law in her struggles with the estate's tangled affairs. Caroline lived at Montpelier with a feckless husband who welcomed the haven the crumbling mansion offered. On one occasion, Lucy's son, Henry Jackson, roused her to try to get a commission for him in the Navy. John Adams, over eighty and in retirement at Quincy, wrote to Thomas Jefferson, nearly eighty, at Monticello, "Mrs. Knox not long since wrote a letter to Dr. Waterhouse, requesting him to procure a commission for her son in the Navy; that Navy, says her Ladyship, of which his father was the parent, for says she, 'I have frequently heard General Washington say to my husband that the Navy was your child.' " The two old men dug in their memories, and both tried to recall who did what in the distant past. Henry Knox, one of whose last official acts had been the launching of the *Constitution*, was fading from the minds of even the men he had worked with, and the public had forgotten him altogether. Only the recluse at Montpelier had him constantly in her thoughts.

Houses encroached on Lucy's aristocratic isolation, the forest was hewn down behind Montpelier. Harry's pet projects were swept away; his ornamental gardens grew ragged, the paint peeled off the house, and the piazzas became unsafe and were removed. The horses were gone, dust was thick on disused carriages. When privation and danger came to the town in the War of 1812, Lucy tried to guess what action Harry would have taken. He had always made the decisions, which she had often contradicted, and they could fight, and she could weep, and then came the joy of making up.

Few visitors came. Lucy did not want rich and elegant friends to see the ruins of her life, and besides, many were dead. Interest for a day came from a total eclipse of the sun; bears were reported in the beech woods, there were tales of wolves and catamounts that killed the sheep and cattle; there were local tragedies such as a child drowned in a creek or a man lost at sea or in a quarry. Her daughter Caroline joined in the life of the community, but Lucy never left the house. She accepted at last, however, some friendly overtures of some of the gentlemen of the neighborhood who came to play whist with her, and rewarded them with cozy suppers and good bottles of wine. These evenings were not shared by the wives, and even today, 140 years or so later, her memory in Thomaston is not kindly dealt with by some of the womenfolk. I have heard people speak of her as if she were a living presence, and the rumor is that she drinks!

Lucy's health declined; then a severe illness when she was sixty-eight brought fever and delirium. She laughed and talked of gowns and hairdressing and friends long gone and called out to Harry across a crowded ballroom. On the night of June 19–20, 1824, she became frantic and her daughters struggled to restrain her, until the tumult was suddenly over and her tempestuous spirit departed at 3 A.M.

Although Henry Knox's name is borne by numerous towns and counties as well as by the repository of the national wealth, Fort Knox—a wry choice, for Harry could never manage his finances—his contributions as a patriot, soldier, and statesman were forgotten except by the specialist. Montpelier was pulled down in 1871, but in the 1920's, local interest began to reawaken. The Knox Memorial Association was formed and built a replica of Montpelier—not on the original site but on a rise overlooking the town. This house is now under the wardenship of the state of Maine and, lovingly maintained, is open to the public. An award for patriotism in Henry Knox's name is presented yearly in Thomaston on the anniversary of his birthday, July 25, and then once more the beat of marching feet is heard, bugles blow, and the Paul Revere bell peals. Lucy is remembered only in an inscription on her husband's monument; she is a footnote in the histories of her time. She made a contribution, however, to the republic she never fully understood, by loving unto death a man who served it nobly.

Diana Forbes-Robertson (Mrs. Vincent Sheean) was born and educated in England but has been an American citizen and a New Yorker for a number of years. Of her several books the most recent is My Aunt Maxine: the Story of Maxine Elliott, *published in 1964.*

A Princely Service

CONTINUED FROM PAGE 54

gan, Joinville was impressed by the corduroy roads constructed in muddy or flooded areas. "There the American pioneer was in his element; the roads were built as if by magic. The cannons and wagons arrived slowly, but they reached areas that seemed to be entirely inaccessible. At night the soldiers did not have an inch of dry soil to bivouac." Here we have one of Joinville's sketches: "I remember having seen a lieutenant general whose only quarters consisted of five or six poles covered with pine branches. One end lay in the water; the other leaned against a fallen tree. He slept there with a waterproof coat spread over his head."

The siege of Yorktown, from April 5 to May 4, 1862, brought back historic memories common to French and Americans. There Washington and Rochambeau had secured the surrender that confirmed American independence. "At every step we found signs of the first siege. Here, in this old tumble-down cottage, Lafayette had his headquarters." During his youth Joinville knew Frenchmen who had taken part in the siege of Yorktown, and had even known Lafayette. He regretted that France was not officially present at this new siege, but he was aware that she could scarcely intervene in a civil war. Besides, fighting with the Federal troops there was a battalion of French volunteers who called themselves the "Lafayette Guards." . . .

A decisive victory at Yorktown perhaps would have re-established the Union. But the clever generals of the South, led at Yorktown by General Joe Johnston, succeeded in withdrawing in time. The Duc de Chartres, who pursued them on horseback, brought back some fifteen prisoners. But the roads were soon crowded. The absence of a staff of officers made it difficult to pass on commands and to collect intelligence. Finally the Federal army entered Williamsburg, and we have another sketch: "All the shops were closed. The inhabitants were standing, for the most part, in the doors or at the windows, anxiously and somberly looking on. Only the Negroes were smiling, and a number of them assumed ridiculous airs of conquerors."

In the fallen city the Federal army was well behaved. McClellan gave safe-conducts to all the Confederate surgeons who wanted to care for their wounded. Although the extremely hostile residents refused to sell their goods, even for cash, nothing was pillaged. Join-

ville admired the fact that when the Southern ladies, followed by their Negroes, carried food to *their* wounded, ostensibly lifting their pleated skirts in order not to soil them as they met a Federal soldier, the latter would merely smile at the "childishness of these spoiled little girls. Others, in their stead," the Prince added, "would have perhaps been less indulgent."

In the valley through which the army marched on its way to Richmond, the welcome was warmer. Joinville never tired of admiring the flowers; magnolias, Virginia jasmine, azaleas, and the hummingbirds that flitted through the trees. At times, on crossing a plantation, they passed in front of "a handsome home, with large windows in the roof" which reminded him of the châteaux of France. Ladies in long muslin dresses appeared on the verandahs, surrounded by a suite of curly-headed little Negresses. If an officer introduced himself to the ladies, she offered him a glass of cool water and a conversation was begun. The ladies naturally expressed their ardent desires that their husbands' and brothers' side would win, but they hoped above all for peace. . . .

Joinville thought that the joining of McClellan's and General Irvin McDowell's two armies would have sufficed to decide the victory and take Richmond, but the Confederate General Stonewall Jackson made a bold thrust that held McDowell back and kept McClellan from striking a decisive blow to end the war. . . . [Because of the fear of Lincoln's Secretary of War, Edwin M. Stanton, that Washington might be captured while McClellan was conducting his campaign against Richmond, McClellan was forced to leave some 40,000 of his 130,000 troops behind under the command of McDowell. McClellan was promised the use of these troops in his final push against Richmond, but the brilliant strategy of Stonewall Jackson in the Shenandoah Valley convinced Stanton that a Confederate invasion of the North was imminent, and he sent McDowell's troops, not to Richmond, but to the Shenandoah. Substantial numbers of these troops did reach McClellan in time for the climactic Seven Days' Battles.]

Joinville saw bloody battles, wounded crawling beneath the June sun looking for a little shade under a cluster of rosebushes, newspaper vendors crying *"New York Herald"* on the battlefield during combat and finding buyers. He saw Federal officers invited by the Confederates to a ball in Richmond on the condition that they would let themselves be blindfolded, both going and coming. . . . He admired the skillfulness of the American soldier: an excellent navvy, hardy woodcutter, good carpenter, and even something of a civil engineer. In the first regiment to arrive, one immediately found men able to repair a mill, a saw, or a steam engine. "I remember a one-hundred-acre wood of century-old oaks and hardwoods felled by a single battalion in one day."

His account ends when the Army of the Potomac is ready to pitch camp to rest at Harrison's Bar on the evening of July 1. [This was the evening of the day on which the Battle of Malvern Hill had been fought. Union General Fitz-John Porter had held the hill and thus allowed McClellan's mangled army to march the eight miles to Harrison's Landing on the James River to rest. And rest it needed. It had just been soundly thrashed by the Army of Northern Virginia under Robert E. Lee in the famous Seven Days' Battles.] The campaign against Richmond ended without a victory. . . .

In spite of the defeat he witnessed, Joinville did not think the Federal cause lost. Compared with those of the South, the resources of the North were greater, "and who knows what a free people is capable of, at a time of peril, when it is fighting for right and humanity?" Such was Trognon-Joinville's conclusion, and history was to prove him right.

A Civil War Album of Paintings by the Prince de Joinville included, in addition to this essay, an introduction by the Comte de Paris, the present Orleanist claimant to the French throne, and an article on the French influence on the American Civil War by General James M. Gavin, former United States Ambassador to France. General Gavin's research provided some of the information included in the captions that accompany the Prince de Joinville's paintings. The complete volume, which was printed in Paris by Librairie Jules Tallandier, was published in the United States by Atheneum.

The Commodore Left Two Sons CONTINUED FROM PAGE 8

the time, Cornelius Vanderbilt was proud of his fortune, and he wanted it preserved intact as long as possible. He figured that the most likely way to insure the continuity of both his name and railroad was to leave as much of his money as possible to his ablest son, who had himself produced male offspring, and the devil take the rest. Undoubtedly his lawyers must have advised him that such an inequitable distribution would incur the risk of a will contest and would create a good deal of unhappiness as well. But this was probably the sort of reasonable business risk which would have appealed to the Commodore, and there is no evidence to show that he ever gave a rap about making everybody happy.

During the following weeks, William denied publicly and solemnly that there was any ill feeling among the heirs. No one could have been very much surprised, however, when late in February, nearly two months after the testator's death, Cornelius and two of his dissatisfied sisters—Mrs. Ethelinda Allen, beneficiary of a $400,000 trust fund, and Mrs. Marie Alicia La Bau, recipient of $250,000 of Lake Shore bonds—informed Surrogate Delano Calvin that they most certainly did intend to contest the validity of their father's will. The Surrogate put the case on his calendar for March 13. In the meantime, formal objections were filed with the court. The contestants charged that the will was obtained by fraud, circumvention, and undue influence pressed against and upon the decedent by William H. Vanderbilt and other persons as yet unnamed.

On the appointed day, Surrogate Calvin's courtroom in the county courthouse in Chambers Street buzzed with rumors: Jay Gould, the sinister financier, was backing the

contestants' suit in the hope of winning a ghoulish post-mortem victory over his old adversary and eventually gaining control of the New York Central; gamblers, equally sinister, to whom young Cornelius was hopelessly indebted, were threatening his life if he did not go through with the suit; most sinister of all, unknown parties were threatening his life if he *did* go through with it. There were even a few kill-joys who spread the word that William had finally settled everything by giving each contestant half a million dollars. Surely, it was argued, William would not allow the family skeletons to be rattled in public for the sake of a few paltry millions.

The crowded courtroom, tense with anticipation of the degrading arts that would be revealed, was stunned into glum silence when ex-Congressman Scott Lord, chief of counsel for the contestants, rose to his feet and abruptly announced that he had been instructed by his clients to withdraw their objections to the probate of the will. Although apparently quite as bewildered as the spectators, Surrogate Calvin recovered sufficiently to admit the will to probate. Mr. Lord told reporters later that he knew nothing of any settlement. All he knew was that late on the previous day he had received a note from his clients ordering him to withdraw the objections. It had come as a complete surprise to him, he said, and, judging from his manner, as a considerable shock. After all, as one indignant but anonymous member of the bar exclaimed to reporters, "It's highway robbery. It robs the profession of a million dollars!"

The contestants themselves were not in court when Mr. Lord made his devastating announcement. William, already launched on the career of bad relations with the press that was to culminate some years later in his famous misinterpreted remark, "the public be damned," hastily retreated to his private office in Grand Central Depot and refused to issue any statement whatsoever. There were, of course, the usual "friends of the family and other reliable sources" who scoffed at the idea of any compromise settlement but were confident that William would treat his brother and sisters munificently once the will was probated and the fortune was legally clenched in his fist. The real reason for the last-minute withdrawal, they insisted, was simply and obviously Cornelius' reluctance to expose the lurid details of his private life to public scrutiny. Cornelius himself, when finally tracked down, was not in the mood to see reporters either. A friend quoted him as insisting that he had absolutely nothing to say regarding a settlement.

Two months went by in which rumors of a compromise settlement mounted. Finally, on May 14, the rumors seemed substantiated when Cornelius went into state supreme court and filed a complaint against his brother for failure to keep an agreement allegedly made on March 12, the day before the anticlimax previously enacted in Surrogate Calvin's courtroom. Cornelius claimed that he had been promised one million dollars if he withdrew his objections to the will. Spokesmen for William refused to comment, pointing out how improper it would be to do so now that the matter was in litigation. William himself was not available. He was on the high seas bound for England when Cornelius filed his complaint. According to some of the usual informed sources, the purpose of the trip was to pacify two of his sisters living abroad, who were now claiming that they had not been properly represented at the probate proceedings. Whatever the reason for the trip, before William could return, Mrs. La Bau was back in surrogate's court, demanding (as was her right within a year) that probate be reopened and the will proved anew. Mrs. Allen, the other of the three original contestants, had dropped out, apparently feeling that she could rely on her brother's munificence. Cornelius Jeremiah could not be a legal party to Mrs. La Bau's action because of his pending suit in supreme court, although he undoubtedly gave her all the moral support he could muster. Surrogate Calvin put the case on his calendar for July 12, and the expectations of press and public again ran high.

Interest in the case as a public spectacle became even greater when the rosters of opposing counsel were made known. In those days, when the county courthouse still provided the nation with one of its staple brands of popular entertainment, legal luminaries enjoyed a public renown somewhat comparable to that accorded today to ballplayers, prizefighters, and television performers. Their strategy in conducting a case, their skill in cross-examination, and their forensic ability were all highly and learnedly appreciated by large numbers of courtroom buffs. Among connoisseurs of legal form, counsel for the proponents of the will (Wil-

liam, two of his sons, and a nephew) were generally rated the pretrial favorites. Henry L. Clinton, their field captain, had distinguished himself for many years in the criminal courts of New York State by an uncanny ability to obtain acquittals for unfortunately situated defendants. A client seen with blood on his hands in the immediate vicinity of the corpus delicti did not daunt Mr. Clinton, and his talent for confusing prosecution witnesses and discrediting their testimony was expected to be useful to William H. Vanderbilt in this case.

The master strategist of William's defense of the will was George F. Comstock, a former chief justice of New York State's highest tribunal, the court of appeals, whose opinions are still quoted. Less spectacular than Mr. Clinton, Judge Comstock was a lawyer's lawyer, ranked by many of his contemporaries as the greatest legal mind of his day. What was more, he looked the part. He was tall and spare, with an impressive mane of silvery hair; his mere presence in a courtroom was said to give weight to his client's case.

Joseph Hodges Choate was the reserve force of proponent's legal team. He was somewhat younger and less experienced than his two illustrious colleagues but was already renowned for the role he had played a few years earlier in liberating New York from the grip of Boss Tweed.

Although the odds were against them, counsel for the contestant were not without their backers. Scott Lord, fresh from a term in Congress, had been the law partner of Senator Roscoe Conkling and was an experienced infighter. Uninhibited by legal niceties, he was a particularly good man in a will contest. His colleague, Ethan Allen, had served for a number of years earlier in his career as a United States district attorney.

As a pinch hitter of formidable endowment when legal eloquence was in order, the contestant had retained the services of Jeremiah S. Black, a former chief justice of the supreme court of Pennsylvania and a Cabinet member under both Buchanan and Lincoln. Judge Black had the reputation of being the most magnificent orator at the American bar. His snow-white, shaggy eyebrows belied the bright auburn wig he customarily wore. Twirling a silver tobacco box on the end of an enormous chain and followed by a Negro valet, Judge Black was a familiar figure in courtrooms throughout the nation. The power of his argument was said to rise with the number of spittoons he filled.

There are three grounds on which to break a will, assuming it has been properly drawn and attested, and when the case finally got under way in earnest on November 12, 1877, before Surrogate Calvin, Mr. Lord made it clear in his opening that he was not going to overlook any of them. The contestant would offer evidence to show, first, that the testator had been of unsound mind at the time he made his will; second, that he had been subjected to undue influence; and, third, that the will was the product of a fraudulent conspiracy. "Undue influence" and "fraudulent conspiracy" are, in practice, virtually synonymous. The usual tactic is to demonstrate that the unsound condition of the testator's mind, weakened by physical disability and insane delusions, made him readily susceptible to a fraudulent conspiracy designed to influence him unduly. In addition to the lurid charges that Mr. Lord alleged would prove the will invalid on strictly legal grounds, he embellished his opening remarks with lofty rhetorical effects of a moral nature. The division of the estate under the terms of the will was, he declaimed, contrary not only to the spirit of the law but to the morals of a democracy. This may have impressed the public but hardly Surrogate Calvin, who was undoubtedly aware that, in the words of one of his contemporaries, "a will may be mean, unjust and inequitable . . . [and] public sentiment and the moral sense of the community may condemn the instrument and its author to no avail."

Mr. Lord himself, of course, was fully aware of the formidable task confronting him. Not only did he have to battle great wealth and impressive legal talent, but he also had to demonstrate that the testator's mind was of questionable soundness, if he hoped to win his case. That would be tremendously difficult. The mere ability to perform an ordinary business transaction was, and still is, considered sufficient proof of testamentary capacity, regardless of aberrations and debilities of the most startling sort. Surrogate Calvin himself was fond of citing the case of a testator who believed that in order to go to Heaven he had to eat Boston crackers every morning; nevertheless, his will was duly probated. Judged by this criterion, Cornelius Vanderbilt, who was still juggling railroads successfully in the closing years of his life, was perhaps the sanest of men. Thus, Mr. Lord served notice that contestant's case would reveal the diabolical conspiracies William H. Vanderbilt had been carrying out for years to influence his aging father. Mr. Lord admitted that many of the charges which would be proved were of a scandalous nature, but he laid the blame for making them public squarely on William himself. The press, of course, was in a dither, devoting columns of space to Mr. Lord's "startling performance," and his "amazing allegations."

It was also apparent from this opening that Cornelius Jeremiah, though technically not a contestant in Mrs. La Bau's suit, was to be the central figure in the case and was undoubtedly the moving spirit behind it. For it was primarily against him that the alleged undue influence had been exercised. As a direct consequence, Mr. Lord said, his voice quivering with righteous indignation, "his father subjects [young Cornelius] to a degradation unparalleled in the history of wills . . . in this will he puts the son bearing his Christian name under a vassalage so odious that every instinct of his manhood revolted against it."

According to the press, popular sympathy was with Cor-
nelius and his sisters, not so much, perhaps, because they got too little as because William and his family got too much. Nevertheless, the will had its supporters—solid, pillar-of-society types who remained unmoved by the piteous spectacle of young Cornelius in his $10,000-a-year vassalage.

Mr. Lord then opened his assault. He called to the stand an impressive array of medical experts who had either attended Commodore Vanderbilt during his last illness or participated in the autopsy. Their testimony was intended to establish that the physical condition of the deceased had been such that he could not possibly have been of sound mind. What it did establish beyond question was that the old gentleman had suffered from a remarkable variety of afflictions and had had a truly remarkable constitution. The autopsy itself revealed in grisly detail that, except for the heart (which was found to be unusually small), there was hardly an organ in his vast cadaver which was not diseased. Yet it had been peritonitis of only several days' duration which finally killed him. Mr. Clinton objected strenuously to most of this on the ground that it proved nothing about decedent's mental condition when he made his will two years before his death and was, therefore, irrelevant.

In sum, the testimony of the medical experts, although it had shown the testator to be a man abundantly afflicted with the physical infirmities of old age, had failed to develop the picture of a doddering old fool. On the contrary, the more ailments the experts revealed, the more the Commodore stood forth as an exceptionally strong-willed old curmudgeon rising triumphantly above his bodily ills.

Contestant's real hope of establishing that the Commodore was of unsound mind lay in demonstrating that he was subject to various insane delusions. Mr. Lord proposed to do this by proving, first, that the decedent had believed in clairvoyance and spiritualism, and, second, that the Commodore had had a mania, amounting to insanity, for wealth and personal fame.

The key witness to the influence of the spirits on the testator was Mrs. Jennie W. Danforth. She was a sprightly little woman, who said she was a "magnetician" or "magnetic healer." Magnetic healing, a heady mixture of spiritualism, hypnotism, and electricity, generously spiked with pure hokum, was one of the numerous branches of the nonmedical healing arts which flourished in that era of bemused wonder at the apparently limitless marvels of science. Some of its practitioners may have been sincere in the sense that they were merely as naïve and gullible as their patients; many, however, were unmitigated frauds. The notorious Claflin sisters, Tennessee and Victoria, for example, made their debut in New York as versatile practitioners of the occult arts. They then went on to greater things, including blackmail, free love, and a friendship with Commodore Vanderbilt that was, according to con-

In court before Surrogate Calvin, Attorney Lord stands between his witness Cornelius J. Vanderbilt (extreme left) and William H. Vanderbilt (sideburns) while examining Dr. Jared Linsley, the Commodore's physician, about his famous patient's mental and physical condition.

temporary gossip, not entirely devoted to communion with the spirits (see "Dynamic Victoria Woodhull" in the June, 1956, AMERICAN HERITAGE). During the contest over the will, the Claflin sisters were frequently mentioned as star witnesses for the contestant, and, when they departed suddenly for England, it was widely rumored that they had been bribed by William's faction to put themselves beyond the jurisdiction of the court. In any event, in lieu of Tennie and Victoria on the witness stand, Mr. Lord had to manage with Mrs. Danforth and her far less alluring magnetic arts.

According to her testimony, the Commodore had frequently sent for her in the spring and summer of 1876, during the early stages of his last illness. These were evidently memorable occasions in her career, and she would drop everything to bring the great financier the solace of her miraculous healing powers. She was equally co-operative on the witness stand with Mr. Lord. She recalled with enthusiastic alacrity that the Commodore had absolutely assured her that he believed in clairvoyance and communication with the dead. In fact, on one occasion he had asked her to communicate with his first wife, Sophia, who had died in 1868. Mrs. Danforth had promptly done so. Unfortunately, however, it had been her sad duty to report that Sophia's spirit was in a very distressed state indeed. To this the Commodore said he knew why and that he would certainly have to make another will to set things right with his wife's spirit. At this, Mr. Clinton finally erupted with violent objections to admitting Mrs. Danforth's testimony, in whole or in part. It was, he said, entirely irrelevant. Some courtroom observers felt it was entirely too relevant to be credible. Surrogate Calvin, for his part, said he would like to listen to arguments from both sides before making his decision.

There was very little legal precedent by which to judge the effects of a belief in spiritualism on testamentary capacity. Isaac Redfield, one of the few legal authorities who had commented on the subject, had written in his treatise "The Law of Wills," published in 1876, ". . . [Spiritualism] may be a species of religious belief . . . but [we] can scarcely dignify [it] by the name of science . . . We believe the courts fully entitled to assume, as matter of law, that what is contrary to the acknowledged laws of nature cannot have any standing in a court of law . . . and that a will which is the off-spring of such assumptions cannot be maintained."

Mrs. Danforth's testimony, of course, did not show that the will was the offspring of the spirits, and Mr. Lord did not intend it to do so. Its purpose was to show that the testator had been a true believer in the spirits and in the possibility of communicating with them. This in itself, Mr. Lord contended, was evidence of a state of mental weakness which would render him susceptible to a fraudulent conspiracy designed to influence him unduly.

Arguing for the proponents, Mr. Clinton stated vehemently that Mrs. Danforth's testimony was irrelevant simply because her visits to the Commodore did not take place until more than a year after he had drawn his will. Furthermore, if belief in clairvoyance was to be admitted as proof of insanity, then the witness herself was insane and her testimony was void. Judge Comstock, Mr. Clinton's learned associate, did not much care whether the witness' testimony was relevant or not; it was worthless in any case. The idea that belief in clairvoyance and spiritualism was in itself any proof of mental weakness was, he said, ridiculous. Thousands of intelligent people believed in it. He also pointed out, with remorseless logic, that there were supernatural elements in all religions.

At this crucial point, when it appeared that the evidence of testator's senility was either irrelevant or untenable, or both, Mr. Lord hastily called for reinforcements. Judge Black, rumbling into position beside a convenient spittoon, commenced his argument by brushing aside the question of the relevance of Mrs. Danforth's testimony as of minor importance. Instead, he launched a vigorous attack on the character of the deceased.

"Commodore Vanderbilt was the weakest of living men," Judge Black declaimed. "He was one who more completely misunderstood all the duties he owed to his own family and himself, and was more utterly ignorant of those principles of natural justice which he ought to have thought of and understood and applied to this transaction, than any other man that ever lived or ever died. And the evidence shows that he was so."

Surrogate Calvin, obviously annoyed and, also, a bit bewildered by this highly nonlegal approach to the question at issue, interrupted sharply to ask what there was in the evidence to show the decedent to have been of weak mind.

"His whole life shows it," Judge Black thundered. "All he has ever done or said about the disposal of his property. He had one faculty that was preternaturally enlarged, and that was for accumulating property. It was so enlarged that it dwarfed every other moral sentiment and every intellectual power. Sanity depends upon the balance that has been preserved between the different intellectual faculties and moral sentiments so that all of them bear their proper proportions to one another. Suppose a man's liver to be enlarged beyond what it ought to be, is that man a healthy man? Cornelius Vanderbilt's bump of acquisitiveness, as a phrenologist would call it, was in a chronic state of inflammation all the time. [Phrenology was another of the new "sciences" popular at this period.] It grew wonderfully. And he cultivated it, and under his cultivation all the intellectual faculties that ministered to the gratification of that passion at the expense of everything else. Morally and intellectually his mind was a howling wilderness. He did not content himself by worshipping Mammon alone, though certainly he was a very zealous devotee of that meanest and least erect of the spirits that fell, whose worship is most sure to demoralize the mind and to corrupt while it weakens the understanding. When this is carried to a very great extent, unquestionably its victim cannot be considered a sane man. His love of money amounted to a mania, which would render any act of his void if it could be shown to be the offspring of the delusion under which he labored."

Judge Black's phrenological approach might have beguiled a nonlegal mind, but it failed to impress Surrogate Calvin. He simply ignored it. In order for Mrs. Danforth's testimony to be acceptable as indirect evidence of insanity, the Surrogate ruled that the contestant must first get in evidence something to show that Commodore Vanderbilt was actually insane at the time his will was drawn. This had not been done. Therefore, the witness' testimony was irrelevant and Mr. Clinton's objection was sustained.

"What it amounts to," Mr. Clinton had said in winding up his own argument, after commenting on the fact that Mrs. La Bau had also been a patient of Mrs. Danforth, "is that counsel seeks on behalf of a crazy client and through a crazy witness to influence this court to let in all kinds of crazy testimony."

Deprived of help from the spirits, Mr. Lord put on the stand a number of witnesses whose testimony was supposed to prove the testator's mania for wealth and personal fame. E. D. Worcester, an official of the New York Central and hardly a friendly witness, told of an employee who had stolen twenty dollars from the railroad. It had troubled his conscience so much that he had given the money to his priest to return to the Commodore. His mission accomplished, the priest took the opportunity to mention the poverty and need of his church, but the Commodore was not moved. He turned the money over to Mr. Worcester for credit to the proper account, saying, "There is considerable good in religion after all."

Oakey Hall, the debonair ex-mayor who turned his varied talents to playwrighting after his political career had been brought to an untimely end by the disclosure that he was a member in good standing of the Tweed Ring, came to the stand to tell the inside story of how the heroic statue of the Commodore, which then decorated the façade of the St. John's Park freight terminal and which now graces the southern approaches to Grand Central Terminal, had been paid for. It had cost $100,000 which ostensibly had been raised by public subscription; actually, according to Mr. Hall, the decedent had had to foot the entire bill himself. These two incidents, Mr. Lord contended, were proof of the old man's mania for fame.

In mid-December, with the trial more than a month old and with public interest commencing to languish, Mr. Lord, like a good showman, suddenly shifted his attack from the public to the private life of the deceased and his family. He sought permission to add the names of Mrs. Frank Vanderbilt, the bereaved widow, and her mother, Mrs. Crawford,

to that of William Henry Vanderbilt as parties to the alleged conspiracy to influence the testator. In support of his motion, Mr. Lord revealed that the two ladies had actually been named in the original allegation when it was first prepared but that their names had been stricken out by Mrs. La Bau from motives of delicacy. Since then, however, such strong evidence of their complicity had been obtained that his client was forced to suppress any such sentiments in the interests of justice. Public interest was revived, and Mr. Clinton was more infuriated than ever. He denounced the motion as "an effort to build up a case by defamation of the living and the dead." It was another attempt, Mr. Clinton said, "to prove impossible facts by incredible witnesses." But it was to no avail. Surrogate Calvin said he would have to grant the motion as he must assume it to be in good faith. The idea of assuming anything good on the part of opposing counsel was more than Mr. Clinton could bear. He was so incensed that he defied the Surrogate's admonishments to temper his remarks. He openly accused Mr. Lord of trying his case in the newspapers by scurrilous allegations because his witnesses were either nonexistent or so worthless that he did not dare to call them.

This was not a nice thing to say of a fellow member of the bar, and Mr. Lord was, to all appearances, genuinely indignant. Nevertheless, it was hard to deny that very little evidence had thus far been produced that would invalidate the will. The contestant's lawyers seemed simply to be piling one scandalous allegation upon another until William Henry should capitulate in order to save the family name. For a legalized blackmailing operation of this sort, the offers of counsel to prove an allegation were just as effective as the sworn testimony of reputable witnesses. The press could be relied upon to publish the sordid details in its news columns as it salved its conscience with pious editorials defending "the sanctities of private life" and castigating those who violated them. William Henry himself was accused of unnatural greed in permitting the family name to be dragged through the mire. But, in spite of it all, William showed no sign of loosening his grasp on all his "rest, residue and remainder."

In the light of later events it would seem that Mr. Lord had really been conducting a delaying action until his star witnesses either could be found or, having been found, could be prevailed upon to appear. But now, apparently goaded beyond endurance by Mr. Clinton's unkind accusations, he unlimbered his heavy artillery. The opening barrage was the testimony of Cornelius J. Vanderbilt, the chief victim of the alleged conspiracy engineered by his brother William. When his name was called by Mr. Lord, there was a ripple of excitement in the crowded courtroom. Now, surely, the skeletons supposedly rattling in the family closet would dance merrily into public view.

"Young Corneel," as he was familiarly known, was, alas,

one of the skeletons himself. From contemporary accounts, he must have looked the part. He was tall and gaunt and badly stooped, and a dank goatee added a satanic touch to his cadaverous features. Even the languid manner which he affected, and which was then *de rigueur* for men about town and scions of wealth, was impaired by a disjointed twitchiness of movement. For him to take the stand was either an act of considerable moral courage or irrefutable evidence that he was every bit the fool his father had thought him to be.

Piloted by Mr. Lord's gentle questioning, Cornelius skimmed blithely over and around the shoals of his mis-spent life. He'd always been told that he'd been born in 1831, so that would make him about forty-six years old. He had lived at home, more or less, until he was eighteen, when he had gone out on his own, more or less. There was no special reason for his leaving home, although his father was rather rough in his treatment and it was not very agreeable to be at home. He simply preferred it outside, and he supposed his father preferred it too. His father gave him an allowance of about $100 a month, and he had boarded around in New York. This arrangement had continued for six or seven years until in 1856, at the age of twenty-five, he had married Ellen Williams of Hartford, Connecticut, a girl of modest circumstances, and the allowance was increased to $150. They had lived near Hartford on a farm his father had given him. He didn't care much for farming. After about a year, on the plea of his wife and her family, the allowance was increased to $200, and there it remained until her death in 1872. Since then young Corneel had been boarding around in New York again, or travelling, or staying with friends, and the allowance had been increased to $250, for no apparent reason that he could think of except that his father was much richer in 1872 than he had been in 1856 and he supposed it cost more for a single man in his position to live in the city.

With the vital statistics filled in, more or less, Mr. Lord got down to the real business at hand. Did Mr. Vanderbilt remember being arrested and taken to a lunatic asylum in January of 1854? He should say he did remember it. In fact, he would never forget it. It was early of a Sunday evening, just as he was dressing to keep a supper engagement, when, without the slightest warning or explanation, he had been rudely arrested and hauled off to the Bloomingdale Asylum away up on 117th Street and Morningside Heights. It had been rather an upsetting experience at the time, of course, and he had not been very amiable about it. His lack of co-operation had induced Dr. D. Tilden Brown, the director of the institution, to admit that the commitment papers were insufficient to hold him against his will, and early the next morning he and Dr. Brown had driven into the city and gone before Judge Ingram to swear out a writ of habeas corpus. William H. Vanderbilt and Judge Charles A. Rapallo, who had signed the commitment papers, had appeared in court to oppose the writ. William, in a most unbrotherly fashion, had told Cornelius that he had better withdraw his writ and return quietly to the asylum. Otherwise, he would be arrested on a forgery charge brought by a downtown merchant, and his father, who lay desperately ill at the time, would surely disinherit him. Cornelius had indignantly refused. He was innocent of any forgery, and, in any event, he would rather be considered a damned rascal than a damned lunatic. There was great laughter at this, and to restore order Surrogate Calvin had to threaten to clear the courtroom.

Judge Ingram had granted Cornelius' writ and released him, and he had gone directly to see the merchant. The merchant had denied any intention of charging him with forgery for what was, after all, merely another unpaid bill. So far as Corneel was concerned, that would have been the end of the matter. But sometime later that year, while he was paying one of his infrequent visits to his parents on Washington Place, the subject of the Bloomingdale episode had come up again. One word had led to another, as it usually did, and his father had commenced one of his tirades of abuse. Corneel had been about to leave when suddenly, much to the astonishment of both his father and himself, his mother had turned on his father and told him to stop being such a fool. Then, of course, she had burst into tears at her audacity, but finally managed to calm down enough to tell his father that it was William who had planned the whole thing. It was not the first time, either. She hated to say it because she loved all her children, but William had always been scheming and telling lies to cause trouble between the witness and his father. Even more surprising than his mother's outburst, however, had been his father's reaction to it. He had hung his head sheepishly and maintained a glum silence, as though saddened by the realization that no man as rich as he was could ever really trust anyone, not even his first-born son. The witness himself, more than twenty years later, was still saddened by his memory of that unhappy scene. He took out a handkerchief and blew his nose. William, for his part, appeared unaffected by his brother's testimony, or by the suffering visible on the faces of his lawyers.

Mr. Lord, with appropriate hems and haws, now broached a rather delicate subject. Had the witness ever been afflicted in any way? With head bowed and voice trembling, Cornelius replied that he had been afflicted with epilepsy in its severest form from childhood until he was about thirty-eight. Since then the attacks had become less frequent and less severe, but it was still necessary for him to be accompanied by a friend at all times. This led into Mr. Lord's next question. Did he recall where he was during October and November, 1874? Yes, he certainly did. He was with Mr. George Terry, his friend and constant companion, travelling about from one place to another. His memory was so good on this point because he had consulted a diary which he had kept then and which he kept now.

"During those months, or at any other time," Mr. Lord asked, "were you in the habit of frequenting the Fifth Avenue Hotel every morning?"

No, he certainly was not. Of course, he may have been there once or twice during the summer and three or four times during the winter. After all, it would have been quite impossible to avoid it entirely.

In those days, in the seventies and on into the early eighties, the original Fifth Avenue Hotel played a role in New York City that no single hotel was ever to enjoy again. Standing at the intersection of Broadway and Fifth Avenue at Twenty-third Street, in the days when the city's life was centered at the crossing of those avenues, it was the Plaza and the Ritz of the fashionable, the Astor and the Knickerbocker of the theatrical and sporting set, the Algonquin of the literary, and the old Waldorf of the *nouveaux riche*.

With a weather eye on Mr. Clinton, who was commencing to fret and fume in his seat, Mr. Lord launched his next question. During those two apparently unique months of October and November, 1874, did the witness visit any gambling house, or gambling hell, as it is called? Before Cornelius could reply, Mr. Clinton was on his feet with a strenuous objection. The witness was not a party to the contest of the will and his habits or whereabouts, good, bad, or indifferent, were entirely irrelevant and immaterial. Surrogate Calvin seemed inclined to agree and requested Mr. Lord to reveal where his line of questioning would lead. Counsel for contestant was delighted to explain. Such testimony, he said, was directly related to the foul conspiracy which William H. Vanderbilt, desperate because of his brother's long abstention from gambling, whoring, and drinking, had cunningly devised in October and November, 1874, in order to hoodwink his aging father. It did not matter that the victim of this vicious plot was the much-maligned Cornelius rather than Mrs. La Bau, the actual contestant. If any part of the will was fraudulently produced, then the whole was a fraud. Surrogate Calvin, after some deliberation, ruled in Lord's favor. It was the first important victory for Mrs. La Bau's side, and a murmur of gratification welled up from the section of the courtroom where the contestant's partisans were gathered. Cornelius returned at once to the stand to answer Mr. Lord's question triumphantly. No, he had not been in the habit of frequenting gambling houses, or hells, in October and November of the year 1874.

"Or houses of ill-fame?"

"No!"

"Or of drinking to excess?"

"No!"

For his last question Mr. Lord lowered his voice to the hushed tone reserved for speaking of the dead to their bereaved ones. How many times had he seen his father during his last illness? He had called at the house two or three times every day during the last three or four months, he replied sorrowfully, but his stepmother had permitted him to see his father only once in all that time.

And now came one of the most eagerly awaited moments of the trial—the ordeal by cross-examination of young Corneel. Mr. Clinton, making no effort to conceal his impatience with filial grief, went to work immediately. There were, as he put it, a few things he was confused about and would like to have cleared up. For instance, had Mr. Vanderbilt ever been in Bloomingdale before his visit there in 1854? Well, yes, he had been there once before—in 1850, when he was about nineteen. Could he tell them a little more about it? Well, he had been down in Washington and he had drawn some money on his father, but his father hadn't paid it. So the authorities, or whoever it was, communicated with his father and he came on and settled it. Cornelius went back to New York with his father and went into Bloomingdale of his own volition. He did not think he was insane, nor did anyone else. How long had he stayed there? About six months, more or less. Well, he must have liked it then, more or less. What did he do next? After some difficulty the witness recalled that he had gone to work in the law office of Horace Clark, his brother-in-law. In what capacity? "I could not tell," Cornelius replied languidly, and Mr. Clinton suggested that possibly he had not been there long enough for it to be determined. And then what did he do? He went into the leather business with William F. Miller & Co. at the head of Gold Street. How long had he lasted there? About three months. Why had he left? He did not care to stay. No, he was not requested to leave. He had left voluntarily. He simply did not relish the business very much. And then what? Well, after his marriage, he had run the farm his father had given him. But that was five or six years later, wasn't it? He supposed it was, more or less.

Mr. Clinton seemed quite perplexed about the witness' name. Hadn't he been christened Cornelius Jeremiah Vanderbilt and not Cornelius Vanderbilt, Jr.? Inasmuch as he was only a few weeks old at the time, the witness said he really couldn't recollect whether he had or not. It got quite a laugh from the spectators, but Mr. Clinton, who was not amused, persisted. What was his real name? Well, his mother said it was Cornelius, Jr., and his father said it was Cornelius Jeremiah. To save any trouble about the matter he used both of the names.

Mr. Clinton now undertook to set the record straight as to the number of times the witness had been arrested. Mr. Vanderbilt thought three times sounded about right. That is, three times in civil suits charged with fraud. Mr. Clinton was not satisfied and the following exchange took place:

Q: Haven't you been arrested four times by Deputy Sheriff McCulligan?

A: I don't know the man.

Q: Would you know him if you saw him?

A: I don't think I should. They are a class of people I don't particularly fancy.

Q: Isn't it true that you have been arrested thirty times? The witness thought not, but he was rather vague about it, and when Mr. Clinton confronted him with the names of some thirty-five creditors to whom he had allegedly given checks on banks where he had no accounts, he was hazier than ever. He could not recollect, he did not remember, he had forgotten, or he would not swear either way. His arrangements with banks, it developed, were somewhat unusual. He had never in his life bothered to keep a regular account in any bank. As the occasion arose he simply drew checks on whichever bank was most convenient and then deposited sufficient funds to cover them. For instance, he had a standing arrangement with the teller of the Hartford County Bank to pay such checks as might come in and then to notify him of the amount needed to cover them. Of course, this method might be a bit disconcerting to banks that were unfamiliar with it, and sometimes, too, he forgot to deposit the money or found it inconvenient to do so for one reason or another.

Mr. Clinton seemed fascinated by Mr. Vanderbilt's extraordinary talent for borrowing money and not paying it back. Under prolonged questioning the witness admitted borrowing and not paying in Utica, Rochester, Cincinnati, San Francisco, and Philadelphia, but he could not recollect as to Buffalo, Toledo, Chicago, St. Louis, or Baltimore. Finally Mr. Clinton thought it would be simpler if the witness could name one city in which he had not borrowed money. He claimed he could mention several, but he would need time to think; Mr. Clinton decided to spare him the effort. All in all the witness thought he owed about $90,000.

Mr. Clinton professed to be highly mystified by all this, particularly as to how the witness had managed to incur such a large indebtedness, living as he did on a small farm in the country. Mr. Vanderbilt explained that he needed four or five servants, as he frequently entertained prominent men in his home; that he had to have an attendant at all times; and that his expenses were very large generally, inasmuch as he was expected to sustain the family name and his father's honor. Mr. Clinton found it most difficult to understand how he had sustained the honor of his father's name by borrowing money from his guests, which he had done. Mr. Vanderbilt did his best to explain that although he may have borrowed money from men in Hartford who had been guests in his house, he had never done so while they were guests. It was a fine distinction that only a highly cultivated person could appreciate, and he seemed quite proud of it. He did admit making one exception to this rule, but he felt that the circumstances warranted it. A man was invited for a few days and stayed several months. He was quite a bore, really, so the host borrowed a little money from him to get rid of him. Of course he had never paid it back. Had he ever paid back any of the money he had borrowed from those who were *not* bores? He thought he had, but he couldn't recollect their names or the amounts offhand.

He firmly denied that the greater part of his indebtedness had been caused by gambling—his total losses for his whole life did not exceed $10,000. In fact, he seemed to feel quite keenly that it was a shameful reflection both on his father's honor and his own manhood to confess that he had never lost even as much as $500 at a sitting. Possibly he had borrowed money from gamblers, but not for gambling. And, no, he didn't think he had ever assigned his monthly allowance to anyone except John Daly, a very good friend of his who merely happened to be a professional gambler. He didn't even know Alex Howe, who ran a place on Twenty-ninth Street; he knew of George Thompson only by hearsay, although he would not swear he had never met him. A man in his position meets so many people. Of course he had often been in Matthew Danser's place at 8 Barclay Street. Danser ran a downtown day game patronized by the Wall Street crowd. And it went without saying that he had been in George Beers' elegant establishment at University Place and Thirteenth Street. The late Mr. Beers had been a gentleman and scholar who had catered to the town's young bloods.

Mr. Clinton was particularly interested in the witness' relations with one Zachariah Simmons. Mr. Simmons in his day was widely famed as a lottery man (lotteries were a

C. Vanderbilt

The Commodore's signature, in the old-fashioned Dutch way

forerunner of what we know as the "numbers racket" and were equally lucrative for their operators). Did Mr. Vanderbilt owe Mr. Simmons any money? Well, he supposed he did, but he could not be certain of the amount. Possibly $10,000 or so, more or less. When had he last seen Mr. Simmons? The witness said he couldn't recall exactly, offhand. He saw so many people, you understand. Mr. Clinton did not understand, and said he wanted an answer to his question. Well, it was fairly recently. How recently? Yesterday? No, he was sure it wasn't yesterday. What about the day before yesterday? He wasn't so sure about that. Before the witness could make up his mind, Mr. Lord bounced up with a vigorous objection to this line of questioning as being entirely irrelevant. Surrogate Calvin directed Mr. Clinton to explain where it was leading. The latter said he could not reveal his purpose at this time. He would say, however, that at the proper time, and in direct relation to his question, there would be disclosed one of the rankest conspiracies ever encountered in the history of jurisprudence. The

Henry A. Clinton, chief counsel of the proponents

Surrogate said he might continue and directed the witness to answer the question. Mr. Vanderbilt now admitted that he had indeed last seen Mr. Simmons on Monday. If this was Wednesday, that would make it the day before yesterday. After further cross-examination Mr. Clinton finally got the witness to concede that he had probably borrowed money from Simmons within the last six months but he could not tell the amount without referring to his books. He did not think he had borrowed money from Simmons to finance the trial, but he did concede that he might have used some of the loan for one thing or another connected with the trial. It was another of those fine distinctions that Mr. Clinton was incapable of appreciating.

"The harrowing ordeal of young Corneel," as one overwrought journalist called it, lasted nearly four days, but he still had some fight left in him when Mr. Clinton gave him back to Mr. Lord for re-direct examination. Where did he expect to get the money to pay his debts? Why, from the same source that his brother William expected to get his, naturally. It got quite a laugh from the spectators and it seemed to restore Corneel's own morale, too. As to his gambling habits, Cornelius claimed, after consulting his diary, that he had gambled only sixteen times in all of 1876, in spite of the strain imposed on him by his father's last illness. The fact that he had gambled at all was due entirely to the disheartening indifference with which his father had received his exemplary behavior of 1874. At this point Mr. Lord attempted to put in evidence two letters which Cornelius had written to his father in the fall of 1874 and which his father had not deigned to answer.

Mr. Clinton himself, during cross-examination, had already demonstrated that Cornelius was a prolific letter writer with an addiction to high-flown phrases. He had put in evidence a series of letters Cornelius had written to Wil-

liam in 1867 during another period of remorse and good resolutions—and incidentally, of acute financial embarrassment. "If you think proper," he had written from an institution in Northampton, Massachusetts, in his rich epistolary style, "to reciprocate the warm and liberal views which I have fully determined shall hereafter form the nucleus of my future relations towards yourself, I shall be most happy to receive such an assurance, and I doubt not that the line of policy which I have likewise laid down as regards the regulation of my general behavior will in a short time cause the many stigmas that now hover around my name to vanish like the morning dew, and that the insane, disgraceful tendencies of the past will soon be forgotten, and in lieu thereof the honorable workings of a subdued spirit and an expanded brain be promptly acknowledged and handsomely proclaimed." William, alas, had not thought proper to reciprocate even to the trifling extent of $150, the amount Corneel was requesting.

Mr. Lord now tried to put in evidence letters from Cornelius to his father, composed in the period of allegedly unblemished behavior in the fall of 1874. In these Cornelius alluded to similar promises of reformation and demanded to know if such promises had not now been fulfilled. Should his father fail to reply, he warned in language of suitable grandeur, his silence would be taken for assent. Counsel for the proponents objected strenuously, both to the admission of these letters as evidence, and to the assumption that the witness, lacking an answer from his father, had thereby been judged a reformed character. Judge Comstock summed up their argument with merciless logic. "Here," he said, "was a son worthless and dissipated. He writes to his father and tells him that he has been good, and says to him, now answer and tell me if you are satisfied with me, or else I will hold you to strict accountability for your silence. Why, the father had no means of knowing whether he had been good or not, and so he did not answer the letter." Mr. Lord took violent exception to the phrase "worthless and dissipated" and called Judge Comstock a liar. Judge Comstock replied in kind and the courtroom was in an uproar. Surrogate Calvin banged his gavel for order, and excluded the letters as evidence.

While young Corneel may not have been an ideal witness, he had borne up fairly well under the embarrassment of having his personal peccadilloes so harshly exposed to the public eye. His testimony, while far from conclusive, did lay the groundwork for evidence as to the great conspiracy allegedly hatched by William Henry to discredit Corneel's reformation of late 1874. Furthermore, the Surrogate had in effect ruled that proof of such a conspiracy would invalidate the entire will. Thus, if William's accomplices could be produced in court, as Mr. Lord seemed confident they could, and if their testimony stood up, it would not matter that the contestant had been unable to show that the testator was of unsound mind. In a day when the courts abounded with professional witnesses who would swear to anything for a reasonable fee, it must have been a harrowing time for William, too, even if he were entirely innocent of any wrongdoing.

In fact, it was a bad time for both sides. A month's adjournment was called to enable Surrogate Calvin to get caught up with other business, but even after this lull, the star witnesses to the Great Conspiracy were still reluctant to make their entrance. Mr. Lord did his best to fill time by bringing a motley assortment of characters to the stand, most of whom were seeking personal publicity or had old grudges against the Commodore and his family. Surrogate Calvin refused to admit the testimony of most of them, but, of course, their stories got into the papers. John J. Ogden, for instance, a hitherto obscure stockbroker who had desk space in the offices of Woodhull, Claflin & Co., was anxious to tell how he had escorted the seductive Tennie Claflin, the spiritualist, to the Commodore's office on numerous occasions and had once overheard the Commodore tell her that he would have kept his promise to marry her but for the interference of his family. (The best he had been able to do, according to contemporary gossip, was to set Wall Street on its ear by putting up the money for Tennie and her astonishing sister, Victoria Woodhull, to establish the only female brokerage firm in the world.) Mr. Ogden claimed that on another occasion he had heard the Commodore boast that many young ladies bought New York Central stock because of his picture on it. All of this showed, according to Mr. Lord, that the Commodore had had loose notions about marriage and a diseased mind generally. Whatever it showed, Surrogate Calvin ruled it irrelevant.

Daniel Drew, once a market manipulator rivalling Vanderbilt himself but now a tottering old bankrupt, Buckman ("Buck") Claflin, the Micawberish father of Tennie and Victoria, along with magneticians and electrical healers, paraded through the courtroom without noticeably advancing the contestant's case.

After several weeks in which the accomplices still did not appear, Mr. Clinton complained about the delay with bitter sarcasm. "Where is that cloud of devastating witnesses counsel promised to bring down upon us?" he demanded. As it turned out, that was exactly what Mr. Lord himself had been trying to learn. Finally, on March 19, at the insistence of the court, he reluctantly admitted that his key witnesses had been mysteriously detained in Chicago, where, of course, it was well known that anything might happen. He told a tale of threats, pursuit, bribery, and other "sinister influences at work to discourage" their appearance in court. In several formal affidavits requesting extensions of time, Mr. Lord revealed for the first time the identity of the witnesses—three private detectives—and details of the plot to discredit Cornelius in which they had allegedly been involved. Then, there had been a rash of ominous

"Notices to Whom It May Concern" in the Personal Column of the *Herald,* a favorite medium, in those days before the telephone, for arranging assignations and other devious activities. The notices, Mr. Lord said, were unmistakably part of the plot.

The effect of these revelations on Surrogate Calvin was such that he decided, much to the disgust of counsel for the proponents, to adjourn the case until June 11 to give Mr. Lord ample time to assemble his elusive detectives.

According to his own sworn statements, Mr. Lord had first learned of what came to be known as The Great Conspiracy in June, 1877, nearly a month after his client's contest of the will had formally commenced. Young Cornelius had turned over to him a letter he had received from one Franklin A. Redburn, relating how a certain "head detective" (Redburn himself) had been approached in the fall of 1874 by a "genteel-appearing stranger." "A singular change," the stranger was quoted as saying, "for which no one could account had come over Commodore Vanderbilt. The old gentleman had become affected with the delusion that his prodigal son had returned to the paths of virtue and honor and would yet shed glory on the family name, whereas in truth 'young Corneel' had never in his life been guilty of greater excesses and prodigality than he was now practising daily." Even William shared his father's delusion.

As a result the stranger, whom Redburn later revealed to be none other than Chauncey M. Depew, felt duty-bound, as a devoted family friend and a responsible official of the New York Central Railroad, to undertake whatever action might be required so that the Commodore and William would be convinced of their error. In short, he wanted Head Detective Redburn to have Cornelius followed until the evidence needed to set matters straight could be obtained. Redburn readily agreed to undertake the job. They arranged to meet the next day at the Fifth Avenue Hotel, Redburn to bring with him one of his most reliable operatives, who would do the actual work of trailing young Vanderbilt. As it turned out, and as Redburn said he realized later, there was something extremely "providential" about this meeting. Neither he nor his subordinate knew the intended quarry by sight, and they so informed Mr. Depew. While the three of them were still conferring at the hotel, however, who should saunter through the lobby on his way to the bar but a man whom Mr. Depew promptly pointed out as young Corneel himself. At once Redburn's reliable operative, George A. Mason, went into action.

Detective Mason's technique, as revealed in a sworn statement he gave Mr. Lord in August of 1877, was simple but effective. Mornings he would loiter about the Fifth Avenue Hotel, a pastime so pleasant that many young blades engaged in it by choice, until his man appeared. It was not difficult to keep track of him after that. According to Mason's deposition, Corneel's day would go like this:

Arriving at the hotel between 10 and 11 A.M., he would proceed directly to the bar, where he would indulge in a few drinks with various friends and acquaintances. Then, with the morning gone and well aglow with spirits, said Cornelius together with several of his boon companions would leave the hotel and journey down to Ann Street aboard a Broadway stage. There, in the shadow of St. Paul's Church, they had their choice of several of those insidious institutions known as "day games." These "day games," which then abounded in the blocks off Broadway between Fulton and Chambers streets, were faro games operated primarily for the benefit of businessmen who worked in the area. They were also patronized by gentlemen of leisure like young Cornelius and his cronies, who found it irksome to wait until midafternoon for the uptown establishments to open their doors. These downtown excursions usually lasted two or three hours. Afterwards, they would return to the Fifth Avenue Hotel for more refreshments and for discussion of what to do next. Would they saunter across Twenty-fourth Street to John Morrissey's luxurious parlors, where they could enjoy a sumptuous free meal before settling down to an afternoon of serious gambling? Or would they pay their respects to the charming ladies to be found in certain elegant, if notorious, establishments along West Twenty-fifth Street? It was not always an easy decision to make. On occasion it took so long to make it that they were in no condition to carry it out.

Once or twice a week said Cornelius would desert his cronies after the return from Ann Street and proceed purposefully down Fifth Avenue to Fourteenth Street, where, as if by chance, he would meet a lady. She would accompany him for a seemingly casual stroll down University Place to Eleventh Street. There they would suddenly vanish into Solari's, a restaurant discreetly and cozily equipped with private rooms, and there would remain until evening. Upon emerging, said Cornelius would be so much the worse for wear that it would be all he could do to crawl into a cab and be driven home.

So it went day after day until Detective Mason commenced to have difficulty keeping up with his man, who was by now growing suspicious. Mason decided, therefore, that what he needed was an assistant to enable him, as he put it, to follow said Cornelius into dens of vice into which Mason could not always obtain admission alone or into which he did not deem it advisable to venture unaccompanied. For this purpose he selected one William H. Clark, an old and experienced colleague who had entree even into the exclusive establishments on Twenty-fifth Street to which Cornelius was so devoted. The intimate and revealing nature of the report produced by this double coverage was such that Mr. Depew, already bubbling with enthusiasm over Mason's solo efforts, could now no longer contain himself. He hustled the two detectives over to William's

office in Grand Central Depot for a repeat performance. William, according to Mason's somewhat pedestrian account, professed much sorrow on learning of his brother's behavior but made only a feeble objection when Mr. Depew suggested that the report be given to the Commodore.

Detective Clark's account of this occasion, in the affidavit he gave Mr. Lord, reveals him as a much more acute observer than the matter-of-fact Mason, quite capable of penetrating beneath the deceptive surfaces of human behavior. Here is his version: ". . . That said William H. Vanderbilt, as he listened to Mason's report, professed to be disappointed and distressed at the intelligence of his brother's delinquencies, but that deponent [Clark] insists on saying herein that there was something in the manner and looks of said William H. Vanderbilt and in the glances he exchanged with his 'soi-disant' friend that constrained deponent to believe, and a little later in the day to remark to said Mason, that notwithstanding William H. Vanderbilt's ostensible grief, deponent was confident that he was delighted with the reports of his brother's infamy, and that said Mason replied that he did not like to think, much less to say so, but that, nevertheless, he had received the same impression as deponent. That deponent afterward accompanied the said 'soi-disant' friend and said Mason to the office of Commodore Vanderbilt. That the moment the Commodore understood the nature of their visit he exclaimed, addressing himself to said self-styled friend, 'I suppose you have now come to kill me and make an end of it.' Whereupon the person addressed declared that the business was not half so serious as that, and when the Commodore replied that he could see through it all, and that he wished to God he had never been born, that said self-styled friend remarked, 'If you would stop, Commodore, to reflect what the country would have been out without you, you would never have made such an unpatriotic wish,' and that the Commodore then said, 'No, I don't wish that, but I wish that this son of mine had never been born; that's what I do wish.' "

His patriotism restored, the Commodore braced himself for the ordeal of listening to Mason's report. He could not, however, conceal his true feelings from Detective Clark, who wrote in his affidavit "that the Commodore appeared to be half-suffocated with the intelligence of his son's depravity; that it seemed to deponent that grief and indignation, love and hatred, and all the conflicting passions, had engaged in a battle royal in which his bosom was receiving the hardest blows. That a few expressions of anger seemed to relieve the Commodore when, after asking deponent a few questions, he cried, 'Go away, go away, and never let me see you again.' "

A few days later Mason and Clark were informed by Redburn that their mission had been accomplished to the complete satisfaction of the "soi-disant" friend of the family, Mr. Depew. Young Corneel stood revealed for what he was. The case, so far as they were concerned, would have been closed forever but for an embarrassing incident which befell Detective Mason only a little more than two years later, or, as chance would have it, not long after the first rumblings of discontent over the Commodore's will were heard. Late in the spring of 1877, according to the affidavit he gave Mr. Lord, Mason was taking a stroll along Broadway one day with an acquaintance. This acquaintance pointed out a person whom he claimed was none other than Cornelius J. Vanderbilt himself. Mason, who prided himself on an infallible memory for faces, promptly said that that was impossible; it was definitely not the person he had followed every day for nearly a month. But his friend insisted that the man they had seen was young Corneel. The upshot was a wager which, to his chagrin, deponent lost.

Bewildered but indignant, Mason communicated his discovery to Clark, and together they confronted Head Detective Redburn with the facts. Redburn, according to Mason, "seemed surprised and suggested that steps be taken to ascertain the truth." Realizing that they had been the unwitting instruments of a nefarious plot, they quickly concluded that simple justice demanded they do all in their power to repair the damage they had wrought. Redburn therefore composed the letter dated June 22, 1877, to the wronged Cornelius which the latter had passed on to Mr. Lord. Mr. Lord must have grasped it eagerly. Here, if ever there was one, was a fraudulent conspiracy designed to influence a testator unduly. He could hardly have been blamed if he had commenced spending the fat fee which would be his for breaking the will of the richest man in America.

During the adjournment granted by Surrogate Calvin Mr. Lord finally succeeded in coaxing Redburn, Mason, and Clark to return to New York. They promised faithfully to appear in court when the case was resumed on June 11. Finally, all that remained to be done was a last-minute rehearsal of their testimony with Mr. Lord and Judge Black which was scheduled for June 10.

That was how matters stood on the afternoon of June 9, a Sunday, when Mr. Lord opened an envelope which had been slipped under his door at his hotel. It was a letter from Redburn stating that Clark and Mason had gone off together, ostensibly to check on dates and places, but that he would go after them immediately and bring them back. Alas, it had a familiar ring. Apparently those sinister influences of which Mr. Lord had previously complained were again at work. He still had faith in the doughty Redburn, but the testimony of the craven Mason and Clark was essential to his case. Moreover, the next day the most crushing blow of all fell on Mr. Lord. It came in the form of a letter dated June 9, written jointly by Mason and Clark. In it they said that they had discovered that everything to which they had previously sworn was the result of a plot concocted by Cornelius J. Vanderbilt himself, aided and abetted by his friend "Simpson," a big wheel in the lottery racket with powerful political and underworld connections. It was only a few hours before writing the letter that they had finally become convinced of the truth. "We agree perfectly in everything," they wrote, "except as to whether Redburn was one of the original conspirators. One believes he was, while one willingly gives him the benefit of the doubt . . . Finally, Judge Lord, we wish to say that when we made our statements to you, we fully believed them . . . and that you could never have had any reason to doubt them until now, when we give you this disclosure. With great respect, [signed] William H. Clark and George A. Mason."

With two of his key witnesses reneging and all of them vanished, Mr. Lord might well have wished to vanish himself. He was left with a set of affidavits which were worthless as evidence, even if true, and which, in any event, were now apparently discredited. However, he went into court on June 11, bristling with indignation, and presented yet another affidavit of his own in support of a motion to continue the case. Annexed thereto were not only the original affidavits of Redburn, Mason, and Clark, but also (and this was perhaps his master stroke which at once demonstrated his own integrity and confounded his opponents) the joint letter of Mason and Clark in which they denied the truth of their own sworn statements. In his own affidavit, after relating the events of the past months during which he had labored to overcome the detectives' fears, and to obtain sworn affidavits from them, Mr. Lord went on to say that he still believed the statements in those affidavits to be true; if the testimony of Mason and Clark could be taken, he said, the affidavits would be sustained. He did not believe that they could be bribed, or otherwise persuaded, to appear upon the stand and perjure themselves, but he did believe that they could have been induced to write their letter of June 9 and then to put themselves beyond the jurisdiction of the court. The close of Mr. Lord's new affidavit summarized the confusion. "Deponent further says," Lord wrote, "that the communication received by him from said Mason and Clark leads him to believe that they have been in communication with some person or persons in the interest of the proponents, and have been induced by them to put themselves beyond the jurisdiction of this court to avoid testifying, and that this also leads him to believe that had they not refused to testify under oath to the statement of their letter, they would have been allowed to appear in court and testify; and that counsel for the contestant, under all these circumstances, deem it their duty to ask the court for a continuance, so that in a matter of such vital importance the truth may be ascertained."

Mr. Clinton objected strenuously to the reading in court of the Redburn-Mason-Clark affidavits, on the grounds that they were entirely extra-judicial. Every word might be false and yet the authors could not be held for perjury. "It comes to this," he declaimed heatedly, "whether this court is to be used only for the purpose of scandal . . . [and] for getting into the newspapers statements which they have already refused to print." Surrogate Calvin said he did not think reputable counsel would resort to such tactics and permitted the reading to continue, although he made it clear that the affidavits themselves could have no bearing on the outcome of the case.

There was a tense silence in the courtroom as the reading proceeded, broken only by occasional gasps of astonishment from the spellbound audience and by snorts of disgust from counsel for the proponents. William H. Vanderbilt sat with his eyes fixed rigidly upon the ceiling, thus avoiding the fierce glare of his sister, Mrs. La Bau, and the sight of the angry fist which, from time to time, she shook at him. Contestant's counsel also read a statement by Cornelius J. Vanderbilt flatly denying the charge made against him by Mason and Clark in their joint letter of confession, and another by "Zach" Simmons stating that if he was the "Simpson" referred to therein, which he was, he denied all charges.

Counsel for proponents came into court the next day armed with their own affidavits. In sworn statements read by Mr. Clinton, Chauncey M. Depew and William H. Vanderbilt categorically denied everything of which they had been accused by Mr. Lord and his reluctant witnesses. Mr. Clinton then went to work in earnest on the affidavits offered by Mr. Lord. He dealt very harshly with young Cornelius, quoting with caustic relish some of the riper passages which contained the preposterous notion that Cornelius could ever amount to anything, and, most preposterous of all, that the canny old Commodore would ever have been foolish enough to think that he would. Almost equally absurd, Mr. Clinton said, was the story of Chauncey Depew concocting a conspiracy in the lobby of the Fifth Avenue Hotel. Depew may have had his less fervent admirers, but no one ever set him down for a natural-born fool.

"The falsity of these papers is apparent on their face," Mr. Clinton stormed. "They were all written by the same person, and that person is a lawyer."

Counsel for contestant were on their feet screaming in outrage, and Mr. Clinton conceded that he was not referring to any known member of contestant's counsel. This did not exactly mollify Mr. Lord and his associates, but Mr. Clinton refused to retract the suggestion that they were being used as cat's-paws by some sinister legal mind in the employ of young Corneel and his underworld crony, Simmons. Surrogate Calvin himself objected to so grave an accusation. He asked Mr. Clinton if he could suggest an explanation for the motives behind such affidavits.

"Certainly," came the reply. "For the purposes of blackmail. Anyone who knows anything of private detectives understands how ready they are to seize upon anything that promises money. . . . These detectives are too keen to swear to anything for which they can be held responsible . . . They have disappeared just at the time for them to appear in court because they never intended to appear. They thought us weak-kneed, and that we would yield to their demands."

Although it may seem now that Mr. Clinton was being rather harsh in his treatment of private detectives, actually his remarks were quite mild. The profession had a most unsavory reputation at this period. In a time when moral hypocrisy was common, when suspicion flourished, its services were in great demand. Nevertheless, it had become an overcrowded field, and its practitioners, in order to survive, had to promote new business aggressively. As a matter of policy, the customer was always right, and their reports were tailored to fit his needs. Blackmail was an obvious and lucrative sideline, and private detectives had been known to prey upon the guilty and the innocent alike.

Mr. Clinton wound up his argument with a few words for opposing counsel. "Why were not these witnesses subpoenaed?" he demanded. "The affidavits are of no value except to excuse counsel for being humbugged for six months. The whole story is a fabrication."

Surrogate Calvin closed the hearing with some remarks that left the whole affair more confused than ever. "What seems extraordinary to the court," he said, somewhat wistfully, "is that if these detectives were honest men and found they had been deceived by Cornelius J. Vanderbilt, they did not make known their discoveries to the other side. The fact that they have departed in this way is full of suspicion."

In spite of his bewilderment, the Surrogate was not quite willing to give up hope of seeing with his own eyes whether such fantastic witnesses actually existed. He granted Mr. Lord an adjournment of two weeks, urging him to spare no effort to produce at least Redburn, who seemed fairly available, or, at any rate, less mythical than Mason and Clark. Mr. Lord, unabashed by the sneers of opposing counsel, resolutely promised to do his utmost. Two weeks later, alas, he came back into court with the air of a man to whom the fates had been malignantly unkind. Redburn was seriously ill and confined to his home. (He lived in New Jersey, so he was not within the jurisdiction of the court.) Mason and Clark had not returned from wherever it was they had gone, and no one knew where that was. Their existence was becoming very mythical indeed. Mr. Lord endeavored to offset this impression with another of his garrulous lady witnesses whose testimony was discredited by Mr. Clinton on cross-examination.

On July 2, 1878, court adjourned early to allow the participants to attend the funeral of Phoebe Jane Cross, the Commodore's eldest daughter, who had grudgingly accepted her $250,000 worth of Lake Shore bonds; Mr. Clinton wryly remarked that it was "the first time he would not oppose a motion to adjourn." But the next day he was back in action again when Mr. Lord suggested that it might be a good time to adjourn for the summer. It would be very unpleasant in the little courtroom during July and August, and Redburn, suffering from what was described as "intermittent fever," would certainly be unable to appear under such unfavorable conditions. Mr. Clinton, by now running a very high temperature himself, objected violently not only to a summer's adjournment but to allowing the contestant any more time whatsoever; if the case were permitted to drag on indefinitely, Surrogate Calvin's term in office might expire, and then it could be claimed his successor did not have jurisdiction and so it would go—forever.

Surrogate Calvin, striving for a compromise, decided to grant the adjournment, but to allow contestant only eight more days when the case was resumed in the fall. He pointedly warned Mr. Lord that there would be no more adjournments due to the nonappearance of witnesses. The lawyer, his confidence restored by the prospect of over two months' grace, took the warning in stride; as the session closed, he was blandly promising to produce not only Redburn, Mason, and Clark but also a fourth man whom he said he would not name at that time for fear that proponents would, as he put it, "educate him as a witness." Mr. Clinton was left frothing with rage and indignation.

When the case was resumed in the fall, it was at once apparent that something new and ominous for proponents was brewing in the camp of the contestant which had nothing to do with the missing witnesses (who were just as missing as ever). Mr. Lord and his cohorts, swelled to bursting with mystery and importance, ignored any reference to Redburn, Mason, and Clark as a matter too trifling to concern them. Counsel for proponents, now more wary and suspicious than ever, were reinforced by Joseph H. Choate, making his first appearance in court.

Judge Jeremiah Black, one of contestant's counsel

The testimony of contestant's first important witness failed to fulfill the rumors of sensational disclosures with which the corridors of the courthouse had been buzzing. It did, however, reveal a rather subtle shift in Mr. Lord's strategy which would, if successful, enable him to take advantage of decedent's apparent belief in spiritualism. The witness, a Mrs. Mary L. Stone, appeared at first to be yet another of the seemingly endless procession of ladies in straitened circumstances who had visited the Commodore in search of financial aid. Mrs. Stone, a serious-minded lady of some refinement, was in her middle thirties; her deceased father, Henry Chapin, had been a friend and business associate of the Commodore. She testified that she had first approached the Commodore in his office on Fourth Street in October of 1874, a period on which Mr. Lord laid great stress since it was during this time that the last will was being drafted. She wanted help in starting a school. Mrs. Stone got no money, but she did get some advice. The Commodore solemnly told her, she said, that before going further with her enterprise she must seek communion with the spirits of her dear departed. He himself, he assured her, did nothing without advice from the spirits. For example, as a result of communications he had had with the spirit of his dead wife, he was going to leave most of his worldly goods to his son William. Mrs. Stone, alas, was so overwhelmed by the daily problems of her mundane existence that, as counsel for the proponents were to suggest later, the only spirits she was able to commune with successfully were those in a bottle. Nevertheless, she was back in the Commodore's office again several months later, or, as it happened, not long after the final will had been executed, to see if she could get her brother a job as a conductor on one of the Vanderbilt railroads. William, who was hovering about in an officious sort of way, told her bluntly that his father could do nothing for her. With that the Commodore flared up. "You can't have it all your own way," Mrs. Stone quoted him as saying. "You are walking in my shoes now. I have made a will in your favor, and that ought to be enough."

"The Spirits made the will in my favor, Father," William said solemnly. "You said so yourself."

"What if I did," the old man grumbled. "It ought to be enough for you."

Apparently it wasn't enough for William, and Mrs. Stone's brother did not get the job. Mr. Clinton objected to her testimony with all of his customary vigor. What it amounted to, he argued, was that Mr. Lord was trying to commence the case all over again even though he had had no case in the first place. The Surrogate, as even his worthy opponent should be able to recall, had already ruled that testator's belief in spiritualism was of itself no indication of an unsound mind, and that evidence as to such belief was therefore irrelevant and immaterial. Mr. Lord, far from reacting with his usual violence to the gibes of opposing counsel, argued quite calmly—some thought even smugly—that, while he was by no means unaware of the Surrogate's earlier ruling or even of the seeming validity of counsel's objections, nevertheless, new evidence, which his conscience would not permit him to suppress, had dictated reopening this line of inquiry. Mrs. Stone's testimony, he added, would lay the groundwork for showing that the will was the product of a foul conspiracy designed by William H. Vanderbilt to take advantage of his father's belief in communication with the dead. Earlier Mr. Lord had contended that such belief would demonstrate that the Commodore was of unsound mind. Now, if as he claimed he could prove a fraudulent conspiracy, that indispensable ingredient of most successful will contests, the soundness of the testator's mind, would not necessarily be at issue.

This shift in strategy was a little too subtle for Surrogate Calvin to grasp all at once. He decided to stick to his earlier ruling that testimony as to the influence of the spirits should be excluded, at least until the alleged conspiracy itself had been established. Getting a bit spritely himself, he proposed that communication be had with the testator in order to settle the whole question.

Mr. Lord was not in the least amused by what he considered misplaced judicial facetiousness, but he remained undaunted. If he himself could not communicate directly with the Commodore, he was now ready to unveil a witness whose testimony about the influence of the spirits upon the old man would be no joke for the proponents.

The witness was a Mrs. Lilian Stoddard, and as soon as she had swished herself into the witness stand it was evident that the big moment had now arrived. For Mrs. Stoddard, to any discerning masculine eye, was obviously no ordinary woman. In her early thirties, with neither youth nor beauty to commend her, she still retained that sort of saucy girlish bounce which, piquantly mellowed by years of dissipation, inevitably inspires in men's minds visions of all manner of delightfully accessible and deliciously depraved sexual activity. Her testimony, as well as her person, was to have an electrifying effect upon the courtroom. Even Mr. Clinton and his august colleagues, though prepared in advance for the worst, seemed dumbfounded and aghast at the story she had to tell—under, be it remembered, solemn oath.

Mr. Lord conducted his direct examination with a dignified reserve that did not permit unseemly prying into irrelevant and purely personal biographical details. Mrs. Stoddard was, she said, the widow of Dr. Charles Anderson Stoddard, a medical clairvoyant who had died in the spring of 1875; Commodore Vanderbilt had been among his patients. In the summer of 1874, Mrs. Stoddard testified, her late husband was using his supernatural powers to alleviate the aches and pains with which the Commodore's aging body was afflicted. Mr. Lord, in his questioning, was careful to bring out that Mrs. Stoddard herself was invariably

present at these treatments. While this may have been a trifle irregular, the manner of her testimony on this point rather suggested that the proximity of her person had such an exhilarating effect upon the patient that he regarded it as an essential part of the therapy.

The treatments had continued in this cozy fashion, two or three times a week over a period of several months, until one fine morning early in September, following a professional visit to the Commodore in his office, the witness and her husband were sitting in Washington Square Park resting from the ardors of their joint therapy when they were approached by a gentleman who introduced himself as William H. Vanderbilt. Accustomed as they were to being abused and persecuted by cynical relatives of their patients, they were quite overwhelmed by Mr. Vanderbilt's cordiality. He told them how impressed he had been by the great faith which his father had in Dr. Stoddard's remarkable powers, and, far from wishing them to cease their ministrations, his only thought was to suggest that a more intense application of those powers might prove beneficial to all concerned. Mr. Vanderbilt's exact words were, according to the witness, "I want you to influence the old man and make him think more of me so that I can control him."

In reply Dr. Stoddard had said that he would be glad to do what he could in his humble way if the circumstances were properly conducive. Thereupon Mr. Vanderbilt nodded his head understandingly and handed Dr. Stoddard a roll of bills which the latter calmly counted and put in his pocket. The witness admitted that she never did learn the exact amount of the fee, but she figured that the roll added up to at least $1,000. In any event, she could tell that her husband was pleased. "This is all right," she quoted him as saying as he pocketed the bills. "I am now ready for business." With the conducive circumstances thus established, Mr. Vanderbilt proceeded to dictate in a brisk, businesslike manner the exact words of the message which he wished to be transmitted from his mother in the world of the spirits to his father here on earth. Dr. Stoddard repeated the message word for word. Mr. Vanderbilt signified his approval, tipped his hat, and went on his way.

Thus inspired and with a prospect of more inspiration to come, Dr. Stoddard on their next visit to the Commodore was able to commune with the spirit of the deceased Mrs. Vanderbilt as soon as he went into his trance. "I seem to have a message for you from your dead wife in the world beyond the grave," Dr. Stoddard whispered. "Are you ready to receive the message?" The Commodore, according to the witness, was a bit shaken, but he replied stoutly enough that he was always ready to hear from his dear Sophie. With that, the spirit of Mrs. Vanderbilt, speaking in the quavery tones of a voice from the sepulchre through the medium of Dr. Stoddard, could be heard to say, "I have a much clearer insight into the affairs of your world than I had before my departure from it, and I implore you, in memory of me, to make our son William your successor in all earthly things. Do this and you will make no mistake. The other children hate you. Only William loves you . . . only William . . ." And as the voice of the spirit faded away, the Commodore said solemnly, "I will do as you wish, Sophie. Billy shall have it all."

Variations of this message from the other world were repeated at appropriate intervals over a period of several months, or, to put it crassly, for as long as the fiscal inspiration from William H. Vanderbilt to Dr. Stoddard was maintained. Mrs. Stoddard could not recall exactly how many times her husband had transmitted Sophie's message, but she was quite positive that the last visit had occurred early in January, 1875. She remembered it so well, she said, for two reasons: first, simply because it was, alas, the last visit, and, second, because the Commodore had been so cheerful. Instead of his usual solemn reply to the voice from beyond the grave, his answer had been, "Don't fret about it any more, Sophie. It's all been fixed so Billy will get it all."

Mr. Lord laid particular stress upon the witness' testimony about this final visit because, although of course the Stoddards presumably couldn't have known it at the time, the date coincided remarkably well with the date of the formal signing and execution of the Commodore's last will and testament. Thus, Mrs. Stoddard's testimony, fantastic though it may have sounded, was a matter of grave concern to the proponents, and their lawyers were obviously most unhappy about it. There was no question of its being relevant: the best Mr. Clinton could do on that score was a niggling argument to the effect that actually the testator had disobeyed the spirits, for Billy did not get it all. Furthermore, it opened the door for the seemingly abundant evidence, which the Surrogate had previously refused to admit, that the Commodore had, in fact, been a true believer in spiritualism, even, or perhaps especially, as practiced by charlatans such as Dr. Stoddard and the Claflin sisters. It was, if true, the only material evidence thus far produced to show that in making his will the testator might have been unduly influenced by a fraudulent conspiracy. Even though the will itself might not have differed by so much as a single stray "hereinbefore" without the advice of the spirits, it raised a reasonable doubt; when one hundred million dollars is at stake even a most unreasonable doubt could loom very ominously indeed. Mrs. Stoddard's testimony was of such a nature that it could not be conclusively refuted. Mere denials would not suffice. Before the proponents could again breathe easily, Mrs. Stoddard herself would have to be completely demolished.

Mr. Clinton commenced his cross-examination by asking the witness to tell the court just how her connection with the case had come about. Mrs. Stoddard said that about three weeks before she testified she had received a letter signed "A friend" asking her to call at Mr. Lord's office in a matter of great importance. This "friend" turned out to be a man whom she had seen around, as she put it, but whom she did not know by name and had not seen again. She said that when she had been interviewed by Mr. Lord, she had told him she had nothing to tell but the truth. Mr. Clinton said he was very glad to hear that, and, if she would continue the same policy with him, things should work out splendidly. There were a few minor details in her direct testimony he wanted to clear up. For instance, she had said that she and her husband were living at 64 Charles Street when they had last seen Commodore Vanderbilt. A little later in her testimony, however, she had said they had left 64 Charles Street about six months prior to the death of her husband in May, 1875, which would indicate either that they had last seen the Commodore in November of 1874 instead of the following January, or that she was mistaken as to the date of her husband's death. But of course she could hardly be mistaken about a thing such as that, could she?

Under this steady barrage of seemingly trivial questions about dates and places, Mrs. Stoddard snarled herself in a tangle of contradictions, and gradually it came out that she did not know to the day or even the week when her husband had died. Bit by bit, Mr. Clinton drew from her the admission that her husband had been dead and buried a month or more before she even knew about it. Asked to explain how such a thing could be, the harried witness said it was because her husband had died in Poughkeepsie. Mr. Clinton, now assuming that air of happy bewilderment which can be so exasperating to witnesses who have been driven into a corner, conceded that while Poughkeepsie might not be the best place in the world in which to have one's husband die, surely it was not so bad as to deprive him of her presence. The witness, by now as irritated as she was confused, angrily denied that there was anything particularly strange about this. It just so happened that Dr. Stoddard lived in Poughkeepsie part of the time because he had an office there. A great light seemed to dawn on Mr. Clinton. "I see," he said. "But you didn't live in Poughkeepsie . . . not even part time?" And with the inference established that there was something peculiarly irregular in the relationship between the witness and the late Dr. Stoddard, Mr. Clinton suggested that it was time to call it a day. He had the scent he needed for his private bloodhounds—Poughkeepsie, only seventy miles away on the main line of the Vanderbilt railroad—and he had four days for them to track it down before the next session of court.

News of Mrs. Stoddard's testimony created a sensation in Poughkeepsie. Even after an absence of some fifteen years, she was well remembered there, particularly by righteously indignant friends and relatives of the late Dr. Stoddard. Mr. Clinton's research into the early phases of her career thus proved to be both simple and fruitful. When he resumed his cross-examination, he knew exactly what questions would unfold the saga of a country girl, originally known as "Nell," who had not waited until she got to the big city to go astray.

While still in her early teens Nell had been adopted by a widower named Coe who lived across the river in Ulster County. After a year or so in this ambivalent situation Nell had come back across the river to "keep house," as she called it—although that wasn't what the neighbors called it—for a man named DeGroot near Poughkeepsie. It was during her DeGroot period that she first met Dr. Stoddard and took to calling herself Lilian. The Doctor had been deeply smitten by her charms, even then well-developed, and they were married at Kingston after a three-week courtship spent driving about the countryside in a horse and buggy making frequent stops in country hotels. Lilian might well have become a bit disenchanted at this point when she learned that Dr. Stoddard already had a wife and family living in Poughkeepsie, but, being both good-natured and realistic, she tried to make the best of a difficult situation by moving into the Stoddard home in the role of general houseworker. This arrangement had lasted only a week.

From the formidable appearance of a lady whom Mr. Clinton asked to rise and be identified by the witness as the original, and only genuine, Mrs. Stoddard, it could not have been a very pleasant week for Lilian. The *Times* carried a special dispatch from its Poughkeepsie correspondent which quoted the genuine Mrs. Stoddard as saying, "There was something about her when she came to my house that I did not like, and that was the reason I discharged her." One thing Mrs. Stoddard had not liked was that Lilian called Dr. Stoddard "Charley," although his name was really "Amasa." There were other things, too, but Mrs. Stoddard did not wish to specify what they were. Dr. Stoddard, however, must have liked being called "Charley," and liked the other unspecified things as well, for he now set Lilian up in rooms on Bridge Street in Poughkeepsie, not too far away from his official residence, where she could keep house to her heart's content. This cozy arrangement went on for five or six years. Then, apparently, it had finally dawned on Lilian that Poughkeepsie afforded too limited a field for the full development of her talent for housekeeping, and, in the interests of her career, she had gone to New York. From that time on Dr. Stoddard divided both his professional and his domestic lives between New York and Poughkeepsie. He also had an office in Newburgh, but nothing was known of his domestic arrangements there. Lilian herself quickly developed a considerable talent for dividing her life into multiple compartments, and during the doctor's absences she became widely acquainted in elite circles of the underworld as the consort of forgers, counterfeiters, and confidence men. At one time and another she had been known as Mrs. Benning, Mrs. Draper, and Mrs. Hall—all names of gentlemen renowned in their professions. Mr. Hall, perhaps, represented the pinnacle of her achievement to date, for he was Edward Hall, the celebrated forger. Having achieved such a position, it was little wonder that Lilian became quite incensed when Mr. Clinton asked her if she had ever been arrested for anything so crude as stealing a watch and chain.

"No, sir," she replied haughtily, "I was never arrested, and I would like to see the one to say I was."

Her "marriages" were usually dissolved by the departure of her current "husband" for prison and were not customarily renewed. This made her relationship with Mr. Benning rather unique, as it had been resumed, at least on a part-time basis, after he had been away for two years in New Jersey State Prison. Mr. Clinton was especially interested in the enduring nature of Lilian's attachment to Mr. Benning, for Mr. Benning was a specialist in a highly specialized field. In the jargon of his profession he was what was known as a "straw-bail man." In plain English, he was an expert in the manufacture and distribution of fake testimony for counterfeiters. Mr. Clinton's line of questioning strongly suggested that Mr. Benning's basic technique was readily adaptable to other types of enterprise.

On the whole, Lilian bore up remarkably well under Mr. Clinton's barrage of embarrassing questions. She maintained right to the bitter end that the number of men she had lived with had nothing to do with the truth of her testimony. Nor could Mr. Clinton ever get her to admit that she had known what Benning and his associates were really up to. There were frequent sharp exchanges between the witness and the lawyer, and her saucy and defiant replies were vastly entertaining to the spectators who now filled the courtroom to capacity. When Mr. Clinton tried to get her to admit that she had visited Benning in prison, she rapped her fan emphatically on the railing of the witness stand and said, "I won't answer any more about that State Prison, so there!"

Mr. Lord tried hard in his re-direct examination to refurbish her respectability. "Abraham," he said, "found favor before the Lord although he had more than one wife." He then tried to show that Lilian had received a wedding ring from Dr. Stoddard when they were "married" at Kingston and that she had entered into the ceremony in good faith. If she had acted in good faith, Mr. Lord argued, she had been more sinned against than sinning, and the facts of her later life, however unseemly, did not affect the credibility of her testimony. Surrogate Calvin was not at all impressed with this line of reasoning and promptly excluded the testimony offered to establish her good faith.

Mr. Choate, who had long been straining at the leash, now entered the fray for the first time with a scathing attack upon the witness, calling her "a woman of the town of the most infamous kind." He demanded that she be taken into custody on a charge of willfully committing perjury. But that was not the worst of it. Steeped in crime though she was, such a woman was obviously incapable of constructing a story which "fit into the crevices of the case so cunningly." Only some sinister legal mind lurking in the camp of the contestant could possibly have done that. There was the real criminal who should be brought to book.

This was indeed a serious accusation to make against the opposing lawyers. Counsel for contestant were on their feet seething with indignation. Judge Black was particularly incensed, loudly demanding that Mr. Choate either back up his accusation by naming the person who had concocted Lilian's story so that he personally could withdraw from such an unholy fellowship, or else retract it entirely. Mr. Choate, for his part, refused to do either, although he did grant that Judge Black himself should be excluded from his aspersions at opposing counsel. Furthermore, he persisted in demanding that the witness be arrested at once for perjury, as he supposed there was no one so credulous as to believe a word of "that woman's" testimony. Mr. Lord, of course, was not silent. He hotly denied that there was any evidence either of perjury or of wrongdoing on his part. Of course, he did not wonder that counsel for proponent were a trifle disturbed by such damaging testimony. Let them prove it false, if they could, before making such contemptible accusations.

Surrogate Calvin, trying to maintain a judicial calm, finally brought the wrangling to an end by ruling that it would be improper to allow the motion for perjury to be brought in his court. In spite of his skepticism, he patiently pointed out the great importance of Lilian's testimony: It was, if true, the only conclusive evidence of undue influence thus far presented, and it opened the way for Mr. Lord to present his abundant evidence, originally excluded as irrelevant, of the Commodore's belief in spiritualism.

Mr. Clinton was quite beside himself with frustrated rage as Mr. Lord now happily proceeded to put back on the stand Mrs. Mary Stone, to tell how her efforts to communicate nonspiritually with the Commodore to raise money for her school and to get her brother a job on the railroad had been so cruelly thwarted by William.

With Mrs. Stone's testimony safely on record, Mr. Lord was obviously flushed with success. He then attempted to bring on a witness who would link Mrs. Frankie Vanderbilt, the bereaved widow, to her stepson William in a highly improper manner. Earlier, Surrogate Calvin had sternly excluded such testimony unless it had first been clearly shown that Mrs. Vanderbilt had actually conspired to influence her husband unduly. Mr. Lord's attempt aroused a storm of protest among counsel for proponents; Surrogate Calvin, highly indignant himself, threatened to

This was Puck's *view of the brothers' struggle over the will.*

hold Mr. Lord in contempt if the offer were repeated. Mr. Lord accepted his reprimand with a sardonic bow. No one could do anything, however, to suppress the jeering remarks with which Mrs. La Bau greeted Mr. Choate's references to the unblemished character of her stepmother.

The trial had now been in progress for nearly a year, and opposing counsel urged the Surrogate to instruct Mrs. La Bau's counsel to bring their case to a close. Mr. Lord, of course, protested vociferously, repeating his stock arguments as to the magnitude of the case and the continued absence of vital witnesses. Surrogate Calvin suggested that he name his missing witnesses and the nature of their testimony in an affidavit to support a motion to continue. This Mr. Lord indignantly refused to do. Those whose names had been revealed heretofore, he argued, had been threatened and bribed, and he could not again permit himself to jeopardize his client's interests by his own naïve innocence of the depths of infamy to which opposing counsel would stoop. Apparently touched by Mr. Lord's impassioned plea, Surrogate Calvin ruled that contestant could continue if the names of future witnesses were submitted to him privately. Such an arrangement was not at all to the liking of counsel for the proponents, and they reacted to it with howls of genuine legal anguish. Not only would this arrangement deprive them of the opportunity to do their customary research into the lives of prospective witnesses. It could also mean the indefinite prolongation of the case.

Despite the comforting assurance that the identity of his cast of characters would be kept from opposing counsel, Mr. Lord's long-threatened cloud of devastating witnesses still failed to materialize. And yet a curious air of complacency now seemed to prevail in the camp of the contestant, as of a cat who has finally devised a way to lure the canary from its cage whenever he chooses to do so. Lord's smugness was all the more evident because it was in such marked contrast to the exasperated anxiety of counsel for proponents. Time seemed no longer of any moment to Mr. Lord as he leisurely proceeded, serenely indifferent to Mr. Clinton's caustic comments, to bring forth more of his apparently endless array of medical experts whose testimony proved nothing except what had already been proved: that the testator was an old man more or less subject to the infirmities of his age. Even Mr. Lord himself seemed bored by them. Then, during the early part of November, 1878, Mr. Lord fired what proved to be his last shot.

It started out like another of his medical-expert duds. The expert was Dr. Salmon Skinner, a dentist who had obtained some notoriety by suing Henry Ward Beecher to recover the value of a set of false teeth he had made for Dr. Beecher's father (and who possibly had discovered that being in the legal limelight increased the demand for his product). Dr. Skinner had come forward voluntarily and was prepared to testify that he had treated the Commodore in 1873 and found his mind in a state of such imbecility that he had thought him to be drunk. More careful examination, however, had disclosed that the imbecility arose simply from the natural decay of his faculties. Surrogate Calvin, scanning the private list of prospective witnesses Lord had given him, was shocked to find that it did not even contain the name of Dr. Skinner. The Surrogate refused to permit him to testify.

"Under those circumstances," Mr. Lord announced, very quietly and deliberately, "the contestant closes her case."

Mrs. La Bau clapped her hands and jumped with glee as the courtroom buzzed with excitement. But an astonishing pall of gloom seemed to descend upon William H. Vanderbilt and his counsel as they sat dumbfounded by the inexplicable suddenness with which the event they had been awaiting so impatiently had finally occurred.

"That is all wrong, Mr. Vanderbilt," Sam F. Barger, a friend and himself a lawyer, was heard to say. "I'm afraid that will give them a new trial."

Disinterested attorneys present in the courtroom expressed the opinion that Surrogate Calvin's decision to refuse to allow Dr. Skinner to testify would not be upheld in the Appellate Court. Mr. Lord himself denied any intention of setting a legal snare for the Surrogate, but his manner rather indicated that he was not entirely displeased with himself. New and important evidence, he told reporters, was constantly being discovered, and it might be just as well to let the matter rest for a while. His client, motivated more by a desire for justice than by greed, had nothing to gain by undue haste. It was obvious, of course, that Mr. Lord was quite aware of the infuriating effect that the prospect of indefinite delay in distributing the estate would have upon those who were content with the will as it stood. Until the defense of the will was presented, and the case decided, they were being deprived of the use and enjoyment of the money they felt was rightfully theirs.

On November 19, 1878, nearly two long and galling years after the testator's death, the favored heirs were at last permitted to commence their defense of the will. Mr. Clinton's presentation of their case was simple, direct, and vigorous. Disdaining to make any sort of opening address whatever (much to the consternation of Surrogate Calvin, who felt that such an omission was highly irregular), Mr. Clinton at once set about calling to the stand a procession of gentlemen prominent in government, finance, and the professions, who testified briskly and unanimously to the Commodore's business acumen, his staunch character, and his remarkable clear-headedness until the very end of his life. Ex-Governors E. D. Morgan and John T. Hoffman of New York, as well as Edwards Pierrepont and William E. Dodge, all gentlemen of distinction locally and even nationally, provided an impressive contrast to the magneticians and shady ladies who had testified for the contestant. Mr. Lord rarely bothered to cross-examine them. The only notable exception occurred when Bishop Holland N. McTyeire of the Southern Methodist Church was on the stand. He had been called as a witness primarily to establish the irreproachable character of the Commodore's widow, whom he had known all of her life and through whom he had been able to cajole the great man into giving away $1,000,000 for the purpose of founding Vanderbilt University. Mr. Lord rudely asked the Bishop to tell the court what he knew about an earlier husband of Frankie's who was still living. Before the Bishop could reply, Mr. Clinton, Mr. Choate, and Judge Comstock were all on their feet vigorously protesting that the question was irrelevant, immaterial, and ungentlemanly. The spectators were in a dither. Mrs. La Bau hurried eagerly down the aisle to her lawyers' table so that she could watch Judge Black more closely as he replenished his chewing tobacco and strode before the bench to present their argument. Even William H. Vanderbilt, usually as stolid as a stone, appeared affected for the first time since the trial had started.

"This is not a trifling matter," Judge Black rumbled, speaking slowly and with apparent embarrassment. "Here is a man eighty years old marrying a woman fifty years his junior, who came here a stranger, after separating from a husband who is still living. That there should have been bitterness felt toward this woman by the Commodore's daughters, some of whom were already grandmothers, and that this feeling should have turned the heart of the father against them, are natural results. But there was one exception in the family. William H. Vanderbilt encouraged the marriage, and continued to show as much regard for the woman as though she had not done the injury of marrying the Commodore in his dotage. But the aggravation is immense if, in addition to showing the distress and hatred that this marriage caused, we show that it was unlawful, and that, therefore, whatever influence Mrs. Vanderbilt exerted was not only undue, it was unholy. There are words struggling for utterance here that I am compelled to restrain, and I suppose I have made a bungle of it, but your Honor must understand what I mean."

His Honor, however, apparently as stunned as everyone else in the courtroom, appeared to be beyond understanding. And so, in a voice choking with emotion, Judge Black went on to spell out exactly what he meant. "That a stranger should sell herself to this old man for his money, taking advantage of that weakness of his nature, is not a reason why a will made under such circumstances should be allowed to stand."

When he had finished, Judge Black sat down and buried his flushed face in his hands. His apparently real embarrassment at what the necessities of the occasion had required him to say about a member of the fair sex was quite as moving as his argument. There was hardly a sound in the courtroom. Even counsel for proponents, though dark with rage, remained strangely silent. But it was all in vain. Surrogate Calvin, once he had regained his judicial poise, hastily sustained proponents' objection to Mr. Lord's question, and Bishop McTyeire was permitted to step down.

But the damage had been done, and there was no joy among counsel for proponents at the Surrogate's decision in their favor. The witness they had called to establish the sterling quality of Mrs. Frankie Vanderbilt's character— probably at her own insistence and against their better judgment—had provided opposing counsel with an irresistible opportunity to tarnish it. Judge Black's eloquent plea, illogical and irrelevant though it may have been, probed through the one weak link in proponents' case to an excruciatingly sensitive spot. However great William's reluctance to compromise with his brother and sister, whether from greed or, as seems more likely, from pure cussedness, he had also to consider the feelings of his stepmother. Her good will and co-operation were essential to him, and he did not dare to risk further aspersions upon the propriety of her marriage to his father. As a lady with social ambitions of her own for the future, this was a subject on which she was understandably touchy.

In retrospect it seems clear (as it must have been clear then to any reasonably astute observer of courtroom dramas) that, by the time Judge Black came to the end of his little discourse on the theme of young women who marry very rich and very old men, the contest was really over and that a compromise agreeable to the contestant would be arranged. Even Mrs. La Bau's vindictive hatred of her stepmother seemed finally to have been appeased. Out of respect for judicial form, the last act had still to be played out, but no one seemed to mind when Surrogate Calvin adjourned the trial for two months in order to catch up with a backlog of other matters urgently demanding his attention. There was, for instance, a lady who had developed a penchant for beating her brother on the head with an umbrella in the corridor outside the Surrogate's chambers in connection with the probate of their father's will. In fact, it has been said that the calendar of the Surrogate's Court in New York has never completely recovered from the effects of the Vanderbilt case.

Thus, it was not until March 4, 1879, that the essential legal buttress of proponents' case was hammered solidly into place by Charles A. Rapallo, a jurist distinguished by his long service on the state of New York's court of appeals, the Commodore's confidential legal adviser for many years, and the man who had been drawing wills for the decedent since 1856. All the wills were substantially the same. William had always been named residuary legatee and Cornelius had always been left with a comparatively small annuity.

The next and final witness for the proponents was William H. Vanderbilt himself. Mr. Vanderbilt was calm and dignified as Mr. Choate conducted his examination in the impressively courteous manner for which he was noted. In reply to Mr. Choate's respectfully couched questions the witness denied, briefly but emphatically, all the utterances attributed to him by contestant's witnesses in regard to his influence over his father; he also disclaimed any design to prejudice the Commodore against Corneel or to turn to his own advantage his father's alleged spiritualist beliefs.

Mr. Lord was scarcely less courteous in his cross-examination. After a few questions put with a most gingerly circumspection as to Mr. Vanderbilt's relations with his stepmother (he seemed relieved when assured that they had always been entirely proper), Mr. Lord said quietly that that would be all.

There was a flurry of excitement as the significance of his words became apparent. After it subsided, Mr. Lord told the court that counsel for contestant would submit their case without summing up. Then, in a voice which betrayed repressed emotion, he asked to have stricken from the record everything reflecting upon the character of Mrs. Vanderbilt that had appeared there by their motion, offer, or allegation. To the bewilderment of the spectators, there was a general shaking of hands among opposing counsel, and Mr. Choate made a great point of thanking Mr. Lord for his words on behalf of Mrs. Vanderbilt.

Under the heading "POSITIVE DETAILS OF THE COMPROMISE," the *Tribune* promptly gave its readers an inside version of why the trial had ended so abruptly. It claimed its facts came from a gentleman described as "one who has been intimately connected with the contestants, but who refuses to have his name mentioned." This anonymous gentleman was quoted as saying that "the compromise was the result of a conversation between Judge Rapallo and the person who has all along been backing Cornelius Vanderbilt, Jr., in his suit. I don't mean his sister, who has stood by him nobly when she might have pocketed her half million and avoided any trouble. This friend of young Vanderbilt told very plainly what it was proposed to show by numerous witnesses not yet examined, and the consequence was that it was agreed that Cornelius was to be paid $1,000,000 and costs of his suit in the Supreme Court, and Mrs. La Bau $1,000,000 plus her expenditures in the contest of the will; and that all testimony of a character derogatory to any member of the Vanderbilt family, past or present, was to be suppressed."

As later events would show, the *Tribune's* version, though somewhat overly generous, was not too far removed from the truth. The proponents, for instance, acknowledged that William H. Vanderbilt stood ready to fulfill the promises he had made before the contest started, but this, of course, would not be a compromise. It would be simply a matter of "free gifts"—the same kind of gifts William had given to his other sisters on their refusal to contest the will. Even Mr. Lord, speaking for the contestant, maintained tartly that "I know nothing of any compromise."

Surrogate Calvin gave his decision on March 19, 1879, two weeks after the end of the trial. While all element of doubt as to the outcome had pretty well vanished, it was, nevertheless, an interesting document. In it the Surrogate took considerable pains to castigate the contestant and her counsel severely for what he described as their "persistent effort to uncover to the public gaze the secrets of a parent's domestic and private life; to belittle his intelligence and his virtues; to distort his providence into meanness; to magnify his eccentricities into dementia, his social foibles into immorality, his business differences into dishonesty and treachery; and to ascribe his diseases to obscene practices."

In fact, the Surrogate said, the testimony showed the testator to have been a man of "very vigorous mind and strong nature, but lacking the amenities of education and culture and a delicate respect for the opinions of his fellow-men." He also dismissed without exception, and with somewhat less rhetorical flourish, every phase of the contestant's case. The only evidence of a fraudulent conspiracy to influence the testator unduly was the extraordinary testimony of the lady from Poughkeepsie, with her background of unusual domestic arrangements, and of the alcoholically inclined Mrs. Stone. In these cases, due to "the discreditable and fraudulent enterprises in which these two witnesses claimed to have been engaged, and their manner of testifying, their discreditable antecedents and associations, together with the intrinsic improbability of their story," Surrogate Calvin reached the conclusion that their testimony was unworthy of credit and refused to accept it as a basis

for judicial action. Furthermore, he urged those directly interested to pursue and bring the offenders to merited punishment, together with their guilty suborners, for, as he put it, "it is not to be believed that a mere fondness for an odious notoriety was sufficient to call these witnesses from their obscene associations unsolicited." (Alas for justice and public expectations, the ladies were permitted to resume their accustomed ways unmolested. Any such stern pursuit would only have stirred up more of the unsavory publicity which the Vanderbilts were now so anxious to avoid, and would, in any event, have violated the terms of the treaty of peace.)

An editorial in the *Times* summed up the whole affair quite succinctly: "The most remarkable feature [of the contest] is the obtuse moral perceptions of the children who have uncovered the nakedness of their parent . . . The worst feature has been its vulgarity."

Obtuse moral perceptions or not, these were happy days for Vanderbilts, even poor ones. Cornelius and his sister may have lost a legal battle, but, from their point of view, they had won the war. Although the fruits of their victory were not quite so abundant as was rumored in the press (the version favored by the *Times* gave $1,000,000 to each, plus $250,000 for counsel and expenses), they were still substantial. All we know definitely is that, in addition to the Commodore's original bequests, young Corneel received a $400,000 trust fund and some $200,000 in cash. Mrs. La Bau undoubtedly received a comparable amount; and there must also have been considerable sums for legal fees and expenses, but the exact figures of the total settlement disappeared immediately behind the veil of secrecy with which the Vanderbilts now endeavored to conduct their affairs. Considering the general preposterousness of contestant's case, these sums were munificent indeed. Even Cornelius conceded, in a letter to the *Times* indignantly protesting against the use of the word "compromise" to describe the settlement, that his brother "acted in a just and magnanimous manner . . . and displayed a liberality far beyond my expectations." The rich Vanderbilts, William and his brood, were happily absorbed with the delightful problem of learning how to spend money as ostentatiously as only *the* Vanderbilts could now afford to spend it.

Happiest of all, perhaps, were the lawyers for both sides. Their combined fees exceeded by a vast margin all then-existing world's records for fat legal pickings. Mr. Clinton's fee was reliably reported to have been at least $300,000; rumor put it as high as $500,000. Whatever it was, he was able to retire and devote the remaining twenty years of his life to writing books about the criminal cases which had been his first and true love. The exact amount of Mr. Lord's fee has never been made public, but he did well enough to free himself from financial worries for the remainder of his life. Judge Black was said to have received $28,000, fair pay certainly for the few occasions on which he was called upon to display his eloquence. In the long run, however, perhaps it was young Corneel's *bête noire*, Chauncey M. Depew, who, although not officially of counsel, topped them all. He entrenched himself so solidly with the Vanderbilt family that he went on to become president of the New York Central and, as a sort of fringe benefit frequently bestowed on prominent industrialists in the days before senators were chosen by popular vote, served two terms in the United States Senate.

The only people concerned with the settlement who seem to have been unhappy were Cornelius' creditors in Hartford. Weeks went by and they were still anxiously waiting. According to a dispatch from Hartford there were 217 claimants to whom Corneel allegedly owed an aggregate of $75,000. Most of them were paid eventually; luckily for them, payment of all outstanding debts was a condition of the settlement insisted upon by William.

By December of 1879 Cornelius himself was becoming unhappily restive in the humdrum security of his new existence. Besides, the mere fact of the inaccessibility of the principal of his new trust fund must have had a most disturbing effect upon anyone so sensitive in such matters. Predictably enough, Cornelius' natural reaction to such frustration was to dash off a typical epistolary effusion, asking that half of the fund be released to him immediately. Alas, William replied that "it would not be a sound exercise of judgment to grant your request, however pleasing it might be to gratify your desire." Unable or unwilling to grasp the idea that one of the chief purposes of trust funds is to protect beneficiaries against the use of their own judgment, Cornelius now petitioned the Supreme Court of New York to remove William as a trustee on some vague grounds of fiduciary incapacity. The court promptly denied the motion. When Cornelius insisted on appealing, against the advice of his counsel, the decision was affirmed with a severe rebuke for bringing an application having neither law nor facts to justify it. The brief era of good feeling between William and Cornelius had ended and was never to be revived.

For a thwarted ne'er-do-well, life without great expectations was a dismal, downhill affair. Soon Corneel was reappearing once more in his old haunts, where by the curious logic of finance his credit was not as good as it had been when he was scrounging along on an allowance from home, and he was again being harassed by creditors, particularly by Simmons, whose methods of collection could be rather unpleasant. He spent his last night on earth in a gambling house at 12 Ann Street, returning to his rooms in the Glenham Hotel at 6 A.M. of the morning after, worn and bedraggled. Early that afternoon, April 2, 1882, while Sunday crowds promenaded outside on Fifth Avenue, "young Corneel" shot himself to death. It seems now to have been an unnecessarily grim ending to a life which, from any

rational point of view, should have continued happily along on a blithe and debonair course.

In his own will Cornelius treated his sisters just as badly as had his father. He left them each $1,000 to buy something in remembrance of him. The bulk of his estate consisted of the disputed $400,000 trust fund, the principal of which he was never able to touch during his life, but which he could dispose of as he wished in his will. Most of it went to his old friend and companion, in good times and bad, George N. Terry. Mrs. La Bau, his staunch comrade-at-arms during the long will contest, was so incensed by this unbrotherly treatment that she now rushed into court with objections to the probate of *his* will. Later, however, she withdrew them after what was described as "an understanding agreeable to all the parties."

Early in the Great Will Contest, when Mr. Lord was developing some of his particularly scurrilous irrelevancies about the Commodore's alleged weakness for assorted females, the *Tribune*, in an outburst of editorial righteousness, had predicted that "rivers of gold will not wash out the stain . . . The name Vanderbilt will disappear in shame and ignominy." Alas for the prescience of editorial writers, the name Vanderbilt, far from disappearing, was transmuted with almost magical celerity into a national symbol of wealth and social status of such potency that later and far richer parvenu families, strive as they might, have never been able to displace it. Even now, when such things no longer really matter, its spell still lingers.

William more than doubled his inheritance, leaving, upon his death in 1885, an estate worth nearly $200,000,000. With twice as much to distribute, he had something for everyone, and there was nothing resembling a wayward son with great expectations to be prudently blighted. In dividing the kitty, William followed the general pattern set by his father. Each of his four daughters received $5,000,000 outright and $5,000,000 in trust, as did his two younger sons, Frederick and George. The two elder sons, Cornelius II and William K., divvied up the remainder, some $130,000,000.

Although this division did not exactly show equal regard for his offspring, there was not even a rumor of a dispute over the will. None of the eight appeared to feel disinherited, as most of the Commodore's children had in their day. Indeed, it would have been difficult to feel disinherited with a legacy of $10,000,000 in a day when there was no income tax and when a dollar was really a dollar.

As a student at Columbia University, Frank Clark could not decide whether he wanted to be a scholar or a journalist. He became neither, but a businessman; he now lives in upper New York State. "The Commodore Left Two Sons," his first published article, was written in his spare time and is the result of "an abiding interest in the foibles of the rich I cannot entirely account for."

READING, WRITING, AND HISTORY

By BRUCE CATTON

On Writing About the Civil War

It seems like a long time ago, and as a matter of fact it really was—sixteen years, roughly, which make up a fair fraction of any man's life—but somewhere around 1950 I got into the Civil War, and now it seems time to talk about it.

Getting into a war that ended ninety years earlier and that has no living survivors is a good deal different from getting into a real live war that is being fought by contemporaries who would like to become living survivors but have no assurance that that will happen; and the veteran of a war that was fought a generation before he was born must walk softly and speak humbly when he tells about what happened to him. But even though death and horror and tragedy have muted echoes when they were actually experienced by some-one else, they nevertheless have their effect.

In the beginning, of course—and this was true of most of the actual participants, North and South alike—there was a blind and uncritical enthusiasm. In 1950 the Civil War looked much as it did in the very early part of 1861: full of color, romance, and the glint of high adventure. Jeb Stuart and his plumed hat had something to do with this, and so did General Lee and his gray coat, General McClellan and his great black horse, Phil Sheridan and his furious temper, and the young men in blue and gray who sat around camp-fires singing the inexpressibly mournful little songs that still send moving harmonies down the years. Part of it came from books read in youth and part of it from the remembered procession of gray-bearded vet-erans standing bowed in a village cemetery on Me-morial Day; part of it, too, from some quirk in the national memory that inexplicably recalls the bright and shining moments and manages to forget the dark and bloody ones. At the start it was all swords and roses.

It began, really, with a great desire to get acquainted with the private soldier of the Civil War. Too many books have discussed that war strictly in terms of the generals: Sherman did this, Hancock did that, and Johnston did some other thing; this general made a heroic assault and that one made a heroic defense; and the men who fought and died at their bidding are simply counters that move from this square to that on an elaborate chessboard and finally are dropped into a box. It seemed important to get at the man who paid for those heroic assaults and defenses and to see what the war looked and smelled and felt like to him.

So my part in the Civil War began, and continued for quite a while, as an attempt to explain it all in terms of the man whom we would now call the G.I. Joe. It turned out that although he was out of reach —on the far side of the river that Stonewall Jackson saw in his dying moments—the Civil War enlisted man was easy to get acquainted with. He was most artic-ulate, he left many letters, diaries, and reminiscences, preserved in every imaginable depository from univer-sity libraries to someone's attic, and he spoke his mind freely. He talked about his officers and about his food, about the irritating absurdities of army life and its deadly monotony, and about the evils of making forced marches across country. (He had a hard time making up his mind whether marching in the rain and mud was worse than marching in heat and ankle-deep dust; the consensus seems to have been that whichever you were actually doing was worse.) He was usually a bit reserved when it came to describing the reality of combat. He was willing enough to tell where his regiment went and what it did, but when it came to saying what fighting was really like he generally picked his words carefully, apparently on the theory that the man who had been there did not need to be told about it, while the man who had not been there would not understand it anyway.

In any case the Civil War soldier is still around, to be listened to if not to be cross-examined, and he makes good company. Rather surprisingly, he turns out to be almost exactly like the young American of today; less sophisticated, perhaps, a good bit more countrified, but still perfectly recognizable, and a very solid sort of citizen to boot. And for quite a time it seemed that no writer could ask for anything better than the privilege of living with this man and describing him.

Taken by itself, however, this was not good enough. The Civil War soldier had many words to describe his participation in that war, and he used all of them at one time or another, often with some heat; but "privilege" was not one of them, and to feel privileged is to be an outsider. So it seemed advisable to go a little farther and to set up shop as an expert on strategy, tactics, weaponry, and the art of handling men; to analyze campaigns and battles, exercising the power of the second guess to show what went wrong with McClellan on the Peninsula, with Grant at Shiloh, and with Lee at Gettysburg. This can be quite stimulating—being a general is easy if you exercise your generalship after all the facts are in, sitting in a good armchair with books piled all around—and it does no harm to anyone provided you do not begin to take yourself too seriously. To be sure, the writer may occasionally get confused as to whether he himself is the general officer commanding or the high private in the rear rank getting ready to take what that general officer has fixed up for him, but aging veterans often do get confused. I heard not long ago about one ancient Civil War soldier who used to entertain his grandchildren with fascinating tales about his part in the Battle of Gettysburg. After he died some of his descendants, in idle curiosity, examined his service record. He had been a good soldier, but he had never been within 300 miles of Gettysburg.

But even when the confusion is discounted, there is still something lacking. It can be both useful and entertaining to provide an authentic picture of the enlisted man in the Northern or Southern armies, and to go on from there to study the way he was used and the reasons why those armies succeeded or failed; to examine, that is, both the chessboard and the pieces that are moved about on it, shedding whatever light one can bring to bear. Yet this sort of thing has been done before, the study of war and warriors is after all pretty specialized, and the analogy of the chessboard is a bad one: it makes a game out of the war, and neither this war nor any other was any part of a game. A latter-day recruit justifies his existence only if he manages to get out of his experience something that justifies his temerity in getting into it. He is compelled, in short, to try to determine what the war meant.

At this point I began to reflect on who it is that rushes in where angels fear to tread. What did the war mean? Well, what does America mean? What does life itself mean—the way it is lived and the terms on which, at last, it must be surrendered? This war killed more Americans than all of our other wars put together; did those men die to some purpose, or were they all wasted? These are questions amidst which one can hardly hope to do more than grope for an answer; yet it seemed to me that anyone who volunteers for the Civil War at this late date is somehow obliged to make the attempt.

He has to do it because otherwise he has simply been amusing himself, using a tragic and agonizing national experience to provide roaming-space for his imagination and his emotions, and also to provide grist for his typewriter. To show why the war took place, how it was fought, and why it ended as it did is not quite enough. Eventually you come to the baffling riddle: What was it really all about?

It is clear enough that the Civil War was a watershed experience for America. What we have and are today grow out of it, and what makes the fundamental question so unanswerable is that what we have and are now are not yet finished. To understand that part of our past we need to understand the present, because today we are grappling with the commitment that was made for us a century ago. The ultimate meaning of that war depends on what we do now. We are still involved in it. When we move to make a living reality out of the great ideal of the equality of all Americans; when we take our stand anywhere in the world for freedom, and for just dealing between all races and conditions of man; when we work for an enduring unity among human beings, whether at home or abroad—when we do any of these things we are simply trying to meet the obligation that was laid upon us a century ago at a price higher than any other price we ever paid.

So the fundamental question has to wait a while for a complete answer. The Civil War is unfinished business. It is still with us, and whether it was worth its dreadful cost depends on what we do rather than on what we say. Enlist in it now and you are apt to find that you are in for the duration.

Or so, at least, it seems to me.

straight they belong to the upper class, but if the marks are small and crooked they belong to the lower class." This distance and direction indicate that the Land of Marked Bodies must have been in or near Alaska. Now hear what Bancroft, the historian par excellence of our Pacific states, says of Alaskan traditions: "At Point Barrow the women have on the chin a vertical line about half an inch broad in the center, extending from the lip, with a parallel but narrower one on either side of it, a little apart. Some have two vertical lines protruding from either angle of the mouth . . . a mark of their high position in the tribe."

But it is above all Hwui Shan's description of the Land of Fusang that fascinates scholars. "That region has many Fusang trees," he said, "and these give it its name. The Fusang's leaves resemble those of the T'ung, and its first sprouts are like bamboo shoots. The people of the country eat them. The fruit is like a pear but reddish. They spin thread from the bark and make coarse cloth from which they make clothing and from it they also make a finer fabric. The wood is used to build houses and they use Fusang bark to make paper."

"*Mexico*," writes Professor Charles E. Chapman, "means the land of the *century-plant*, just as 'Fusang' was named for the 'Fusang tree.' In no other country in the world is there a plant put to such uses as those described by Hwui Shan. . . . The sprouts of the century-plant do resemble those of the bamboo and the people do eat them. The plant does furnish a rough sort of thread from which a kind of hempen cloth is made and also a fine variety resembling linen. Furthermore, paper is made from . . . the fibre." He might have added that the century plant, or *maguey* as it is called in Mexico (*genus Agave* in Latin), is often described by travellers as a tree. As residents of our southwestern states are aware, it sends up a tall, branching, beautifully flowered, candelabralike stalk that often reaches a height of thirty feet. It was widely cultivated in regular groves in ancient Mexico, its trunk being used for the beams and rafters of buildings and its broad, flat, waterproof, cactuslike leaves for the walls and roofs. On his return to China, Hwui Shan presented the Emperor with three hundred pounds of "silk" from the Fusang tree and also gave him "a kind of semi-transparent stone, about a foot in circumference, cut in the form of a mirror," a curious item that sounds exactly like one of the polished obsidian (volcanic glass) mirrors used by the ancient Mexicans.

"They have a system of writing," his report continues. "But they have no fortresses or walled cities, no military weapons or soldiers and they do not wage war in that kingdom."

As pointed out by Ignacio Bernal in his recent *Mexico Before Cortez*, the period of Hwui Shan's voyage—458-499 A.D.—coincided with a golden age in Mexico now called by archaeologists the Classic Period. The Mexicans of that age possessed a system of hieroglyphic writing undeciphered to this day; a calendar more accurate than our own; and a knowledge of mathematics that included a symbol for zero centuries before the concept was known in Europe. They also built great metropolitan cities, particularly one named Teotihuacán in the ruins of which, twenty-five miles from Mexico City, may be seen the gigantic Pyramid of the Sun. These extraordinary metropolises (not to be confused with the Aztec cities that were there at the time of the Spanish conquest) are unique in the history of ancient cultures, for they had no city walls or fortifications. Their inhabitants appear to have had no enemies—and hence no need to defend themselves—and to have known nothing about war. They worshipped peaceful gods like the sun and the moon and the rain and the gentle Quetzalcoatl, the winged serpent, to whom butterflies were offered in sacrifice. It was not until the Toltec period (and much later still, in the time of the relatively modern Aztecs) that bloodthirsty warriors who practiced human sacrifice conquered and ruled the country. Another unusual thing about the Mexicans of the Classic Period is that they cremated their dead, a practice unheard of at any other time in Mexican history and one pertinent to the question of Buddhist influence.

"The ground contains no iron," said Hwui Shan, "but it has copper. The people do not value gold and silver."

Iron, of course, existed in Mexico but its use was unknown before the time of the Spaniards, who were the first to mine it. "Metals never had a great importance in American cultures," writes Dr. Bernal. "Metals were for luxury rather than for their practical usefulness. Nevertheless, especially among the Tarascos, copper was abundantly used to make needles, pliers, awls, hatchets, and the cutting edges of farm tools." The Tarascos, incidentally, were a tribe who lived in western Mexico, the region where Hwui Shan would have landed. His reference to the Mexicans' indifference toward gold and silver is also borne out by eyewitness accounts of the Spaniards. Bernal Díaz, one of Cortés' lieutenants, describing the market place of Mexico City (in his *Discovery and Conquest of*

Mexico), stated that gold and silver, far from being used as money, were bought and sold like other commodities and paid for with the regular currency of the country, which was cocoa.

Hwui Shan's report also contains information about the emperor and the noblemen of Fusang, about slavery, crime and a prison system for punishing criminals, marriage, funeral customs, etcetera. Much of this data cannot be checked because of the lack of literature surviving from the Classic Period and our inability to decipher its hieroglyphs, but some of it, frankly, has a suspiciously Oriental, even a Chinese, sound: for example, the visitor wrote that the emperor of Fusang changed the color of his clothes at certain seasons of the year, from blue to red, then yellow, white, and black.

There are also some serious inconsistencies and problems in Hwui Shan's story. The century plant does not bear reddish, pear-shaped fruit; moreover, objectors say that any convincing description of the plant should have included a reference to *pulque*, the well-known Mexican liquor made from its juice. A

a lot among themselves but were shy when they saw ordinary human beings. They gave birth to their young after six or seven months of pregnancy and nursed them on their backs. The babies were able to walk within 100 days and were fully grown in three or four years. "Believe it or not," he concluded, "this is true!"

Problems like these may cause some readers to dismiss the entire story of Hwui Shan as nothing more than a fifth-century addition to the old Chinese fairy tale of Fusang. It ought to be remembered, however, that very few ancient travellers who visited foreign countries for the first time were accurate in everything they reported, nor were their accounts lacking in fantastic touches. Take, for example, the Icelandic sagas that tell of the colony of Vinland. They not only mention monopeds—one-legged men—but recount such bloodcurdling Viking exploits as that of Freydís, Leif Ericson's half sister, who on one expedition to the New World allegedly murdered all the other women in her party with a battle axe in order to retain supreme command. For centuries, such tall tales as these

Decorative architectural details from Asia and America show striking similarities. The one at left, dating from the second century A.D., comes from southern India, an area which strongly influenced Hindu-Buddhist art throughout Southeast Asia. The one at right, from Chichén Itzá in Mexico, is the product of a civilization that flourished in Hwui Shan's lifetime. Both combine a lotus design with living figures—a fish (left) and a human being (right).

particularly difficult problem also appears in one excerpt which has been said to prove that the Land of Fusang was not in America: "They have large cattle horns which they use as containers, the biggest ones holding about five gallons. They have carts drawn by horses, cattle, and deer. The people of that country raise deer as the Chinese raise cattle and from their milk make a fermented liquor. . . ." It is well known, of course, that American Indians, in spite of the high degree of civilization they reached in Mexico and other places, never domesticated animals or, strange to say, discovered the use of the wheel, except as they used it in toys. Cattle and horses and carts—not to mention trained deer!—were unknown among them until the Spaniards introduced them.

There is also another difficult problem involved in Hwui Shan's account—his mention of a Land of Women. This, he said, was located 1,000 li beyond the Land of Fusang. Its female inhabitants were completely covered with hair, walked erect, and chattered

caused the sagas to be regarded as entirely fictitious. Marco Polo, the first Westerner to see the Far East, lived for twenty years at the court of Kubla Khan and travelled widely in Asia. He came back to Venice with Paul Bunyan-like tales of a bird that could lift an elephant (the roc of the *Arabian Nights,* which he had heard about and accepted as factual), oxen as large as elephants, dogs as big as donkeys, and men with tails. Christopher Columbus, besides being a superb navigator, was a geographer and a cartographer of distinction, one of the first mariners to use the compass, and the very first to note that the North Star moves around the celestial pole. Yet even this sophisticated man repeated, like Hwui Shan, the story of an Island of Amazons. As a matter of fact, the legend of a Land of Women plays a considerable role in American history. California was long believed by the Spaniards to be an island rich in pearls and gold, populated by black-skinned ladies "without a single man among them" and ruled by a beautiful queen

Though widely separated in time, these two pottery bowls—the one at left from prehistoric China, the one at right found at Whitewater, New Mexico, and dating from the tenth century A.D.—are similar not only in the stick-like human figure prominent in the design, but in the potters' techniques.

"of majestic proportions" named Calafía. Such was the description of our as-yet-undiscovered Golden State in *Amadis of Gaul*, that infamous five-volume, fifteenth-century best seller (with sequels) which, more than any other book, was responsible for the madness of Don Quixote. The legend inspired the equipping of expeditions and persisted as late as the seventeenth century. So, too, did the belief of brave, strong men in the Fountain of Youth, the Earthly Paradise, and the fabulous Golden Kingdom of Quivira.

Compared with other travellers Hwui Shan does not seem such a Munchausen. In fact, his story is exceptionally free, as ancient stories of discovery go, from the marvelous and the incredible. Nevertheless, as I have suggested, it does have problems. Since 1761, when the Chevalier de Guignes encountered it in *The Records of the Liang Dynasty* and brought it to the attention of Western scholars for the first time, it has engendered a lively and somewhat belligerent controversy, mostly during the nineteenth century, among savants in Europe and America. Significantly, those who have believed that Hwui Shan discovered America—at least those who have written to that effect—have outnumbered their opponents two to one. Besides those already mentioned they include José Perez, Gustave d'Eichthal, Dr. A. Gordon, the Reverend N. W. Jones, the Abbé Brasseur de Bourbourg, and the Marquis d'Hervey de Saint-Denys. But those opposed —Lucien Adam, Vivien de Saint-Martin, Dr. E. Bretschneider, and Professor S. W. Williams—had a formidable leader in the person of Heinrich Julius Klaproth, a celebrated Sinologue of the early nineteenth century, who wrote a critical paper on Hwui Shan in 1831. Klaproth and his followers did not deny the fact of the missionary's voyage but disputed its length and its destination. They maintained that the distance had been falsified, either through the braggadocio or Buddhist zeal of the adventurous missionary himself or else by the courtiers who questioned him, the his-

torians who published the record, or the scribes who copied and recopied the original documents. Scribal errors were common enough, of course, in the days before printing (an art invented in China, but not until the ninth century); they were particularly apt to occur where numbers were involved.

The question then arises: If Fusang was not in North America, where was it? Klaproth's theory (the only one that has ever been advanced by the opposition) was that Hwui Shan must have reached some country close to China—probably, because it lies in a generally easterly direction, Japan.

Unfortunately for the fame of our Buddhist Columbus, Hubert Howe Bancroft, that astonishing academic entrepreneur who founded The History Company, Incorporated, of San Francisco and successfully applied commercial business methods to the wholesale buying, writing, and selling of history, inclined to Klaproth's view, a fact that above all others explains why the subject has been ignored by so many American historians. Yet Bancroft remained intrigued by Hwui Shan. He quoted a large part of the Chinese text in his *Native Races of the Pacific States,* published in 1886, and gave a great deal of help and encouragement to Edward P. Vining, whose *An Inglorious Columbus,* dedicated to Bancroft, still remains the most impressive work on the voyage of Hwui Shan. Vining's book is unshaken—indeed, its conclusions seem to be confirmed—by recent archaeological studies; though not the last book to be written on the subject, it seems to have put an end to the controversy.

The charge has also been made that Klaproth was guilty of conduct unbecoming a scholar: that he took up the opposition through chagrin that his rival, de Guignes, had been the first to discover Hwui Shan. Indeed, the Japan theory does not do justice to Klaproth's reputation. It is well known that the Chinese had contacts with Japan as early as the first century A.D. and possessed a written history of that country in the year 297, nearly two centuries before Hwui Shan. Many known details concerning Japan also make it abundantly clear that he could not have mistaken Japan for Fusang: iron was used in Japan at an early period, the Japanese were anything but pacifistic (in Hwui Shan's time they were engaged in a military invasion of Korea), and the introduction of Buddhism there by other missionaries in 552 A.D., long after Hwui Shan's death, is well documented. It seems hardly necessary to add that Japan is actually mentioned in Hwui Shan's narrative in connection with locating the Land of Marked Bodies, or that the possibility of errors in ancient manuscripts is a knife that cuts both ways.

What about the reddish, pear-shaped fruit of the

Fusang tree? Vining and Chapman thought it may not have been the century plant at all but the prickly pear or cactus apple, known in Mexico as the *tuna*, which grows there on a cactus similar in some respects to the century plant; travellers sometimes confuse the two. And the Mexicans did not drink *pulque,* Dr. Bernal informs us, until the tenth century, 500 years after Hwui Shan. The trained deer are obviously reindeer—transplanted, perhaps, from Hwui Shan's journey to Siberia and misrepresented by the Chinese scribes, who recorded his story, as drawing carts instead of sleighs. Gigantic cattle horns, probably those of prehistoric bison which once roamed Mexico, were shown as curios by Montezuma to Cortés and have also been found in ruins in Mexico, indicating that they were indeed used as containers. In fact, almost all the inconsistencies and problems in Hwui Shan's story are open to interpretation and have a way of turning out in his favor. For instance, Vining has expertly shown, while performing what is probably one of the neatest tricks in all scholarship, that the shy, chattering, hairy "ladies" of the Land of Women—with their precocious children—who lived 1,000 li beyond Fusang, were Central American monkeys.

Regarding the prison system of Fusang, Vining thought that Hwui Shan's statements are possibly not to be taken literally but as an allegory on the Buddhist doctrine on hell. This brings up again the question of Buddhist influence on the religious beliefs of early American civilizations and Hwui Shan's statement that he and his companions introduced it into Fusang. That question almost seems to be directly answered by the Austrian anthropologist Dr. Robert Heine-Geldern, who—writing quite independently of the subject of Hwui Shan—has stated: "We have little doubt that a comparative analysis of the Mexican Mayan religion will reveal many traces of the former influences of Hinduism or Buddhism or both. To mention but one instance, the conceptions of hell and the punishments inflicted there resemble Buddhist and Hindu beliefs to such an extent that the assumption of historic relationship is almost inevitable."

Who will now revive the Hwui Shan controversy and gainsay the conclusion of Dr. Charles E. Chapman, the last American historian to write on the subject: "Either Fusang was in America, presumably in Mexico, or else the story was a lie. The evidence that it was true is almost overwhelming"?

Robert Larson, who lives in Hollywood, has had a varied career as artist, scene designer, journalist, motion-picture animator, and studio executive. In recent years he has devoted himself to scholarly pursuits, and is now engaged in research on the early history of Los Angeles. Illustrations on pages 107–108 are reprinted by permission of Alfred A. Knopf, Inc., from The Eagle, the Jaguar & the Serpent *by Miguel Covarrubias. Copyright 1954 by Miguel Covarrubias.*

"*God, please get us out of this*" CONTINUED FROM PAGE 51

"For what?" another asked. No answer.

We had turned off the light to conserve the batteries. The voice was right: unnecessary talking would use up the air, so we remained silent in the darkness. The men settled back with their thoughts. I lay curled up on a piece of metal overhang. Others sat on the half-submerged ladder or against the upper bulkhead. Although we were upside down, the ship was not quite perpendicular to the bottom. There was an angle of thirty degrees or so. We were fortunate in that respect: we could keep out of the water somewhat.

Only a short time had passed since the bugle had called us to action, and my watch was still ticking. The ship must have gone down in fifteen minutes. It happened too quickly for us to have known much fear, too quickly for us to get out. On the other hand, it had seemed like a lifetime.

Time crawled. The water rose slowly as the air was used, steadily pushing its way into the broken ship. The bodies of our shipmates bobbed against the handling-room entrance to the passageway. It seemed as if they wanted to join the living there. We moved them behind some wreckage. There was nothing we could do for them, nor they for us. Sooner or later we would join our dead comrades. Perhaps others were joining me in my silent prayer, "God, please get us out of this."

The taste and smell of fuel oil was sickening. Occasionally a man would move off, determined to seek some way of escape. None returned, however. But each man's life was all he had, and he was entitled to try to save it as best he could.

There were less than twenty of us left, but, incredibly, there was no panic. The hours passed by. The water level rose inexorably, inch by awful inch. I thought of home. Days of growing up. People I had known. Long summer days of hard farm work, but with lots of time for fun. Swimming, fishing. Pleasant thoughts. Even now, in the darkness, the memories brought a smile. My family. They were a source of strength to me.

It had been more than a year since I had seen them. They had all waved goodbye as I walked out of the yard that morning. How would they take the news of my death? With sadness, certainly, but with a reserved pride. I hoped they would be all right.

My watch stopped finally. Time did not matter. I dropped it in the water with a splash. Then I took out a pocketful of change and dropped the coins absently into the water. There was a place in town where *Oklahoma* sailors met to drink beer, sing songs of the Navy, tell sea stories, dance with their girls, laugh, and fight with sailors from other ships. Remembering it, I couldn't resist saying aloud, "How about a cold beer? I'm thirsty."

"Set 'em up, all the way around," a sailor replied.

"Join the Navy and see the world—from the bottom of Pearl Harbor."

No one seemed to mind the wise-cracks. It was crazy, maybe, but every-one seemed to relax a bit.

The hours moved on. It was prob-ably dark above us now, and it seemed darker here, somehow.

Breaking another long silence, one of the men recalled that there was an escape hatch here. "It's narrow and goes straight down, thirty feet or so to the main deck. Let's give it a try." I had to orient myself because "up" was now "down," and we were actually sitting on the overhead. I hadn't even known there was such a hatch right here. We turned on the light.

However, since it was more than three decks down the hatch, all under water, across the main deck and then up to the surface, escape did not seem probable. No one could hold his breath that long, and there might very well be obstructions, too. The hatch was only as big around as a man's body. But we had nothing to lose and any action was welcome. A man volun-teered to try. We took off our skivvy shirts and made a sort of life line to guide him back. "So long," he said. He disappeared and did not return. Other men tried, but none of them re-turned. Soon the skivvy-shirt string hung slack. I decided to wait, although I didn't know why. It was as if someone had told me to wait, because somehow I was not afraid.

Time went by. As the water rose, the air became more and more foul. I felt a longing to break the silence again.

"Willy," I said, "I'll bet you a dollar we'll suffocate before we drown." "Okay, you're on," agreed Willy. "I say we drown first." We each produced a soggy dollar bill, after which we lapsed again into silence.

Once we heard firing way above us; it sounded strange coming down through the water in the darkness and the silence. I tried to imagine what was going on up there. It must be night, because more than half a day had passed. The Japs had really caught us napping, but that was the extent of our knowledge. We had seen nothing before the *Oklahoma* went down. Had the other ships also been sunk? Were the Japanese landing troops? Not knowing was terrible.

My thoughts were kaleidoscopic—school, family, my Navy life. I thought of pretty girls, laughing, full of life. I felt terribly alone, and blurted, "Damn it, I'm not even twenty and I'll never know or love a girl again!" At that moment this loss seemed stronger than any other. No one said anything, pre-sumably out of silent agreement.

"It's getting worse," a voice said out of the dark, "we'll have to move. The Lucky Bag compartment [the ship's lost-and-found locker] is right next to us. Let's try to get in there if it isn't flooded."

This compartment went nowhere, but at least it would be more comfort-able, with stacks of mattresses and pea-coats to lie on. We turned on the flash-light and tested for air through a hole in the compartment bulkhead. There was no evidence of water so we opened the hatch and moved in. I kicked off my shoes and stretched out on a pile of clothing, lying there in what re-mained of the uniform of the day—oil-stained shorts. The dollar bill was safely tucked away in my watch pocket. I lay next to the bulkhead, along the slant of the deck, feet toward the water in the lower part of the compartment. It was rising slowly.

Sudden shouts through the bulkhead told us there was another group like

ours in the adjoining space. We talked to them, briefly. Their situation was similar to ours; they, too, were trapped.

Water lapped over the hatch open-ing into the passageway. By now, we were only vaguely aware of time as we fell again into silence. Each of us was alone with himself in our living tomb.

Suddenly, anger rumbled within me. Why couldn't we have died in the sun where we could have met death head on? That was the way to die, on your feet, like a man. But instead, it was to be a slow, useless death, imprisoned in our dark iron cell.

Still, perhaps to die like this required a special kind of courage. Could I meet the test? "Oh, God," I prayed, "re-lieve us of our torment. If it is Your will that we die here, please watch over our families and comfort them. We are delivered unto You and ask to be for-given for our sins."

The hours passed . . .

Unexpectedly, and from a great dis-tance, came the sound of hammering. Metal against metal! Our hearts jumped. The sound stopped, and we held our breaths. It started again, closer, and died away once more.

"What is it?" someone asked. "Is it possible they can reach us?"

"No. I don't know," another said. "Quiet. Listen."

We looked around, not seeing any-thing in the dark, of course, but look-ing anyway. Ears strained for the sound to begin once more. It seemed an eter-nity. Was help on the way? Then the noise began again, not sporadically, but like the knock of an automatic tool. Did it mean rescuers? Why was the sound fainter now? It stopped again. Were they unable to find a route to us through the sunken ship? I dared not hope, but my heart pounded.

We hammered at the steel bulkhead with a dog wrench. Three dots—three dashes—three dots—SOS!!

We must let them know we're here. It had to be a pneumatic air hammer! It had to be! Or were the spaces over us and under us so flooded that we were sealed away? There it was again.

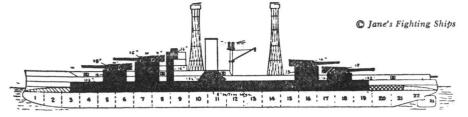

When the Japanese attacked, the doors between the Oklahoma's *below-decks compartments were open for an inspection next day. There was no time to set "Condition Zed"—complete watertight integrity; once torpedoes had breached her hull, she flooded quickly. Armor protected only those areas shown in black.*

Louder! Much louder now. Then, suddenly, silence.

"They're trying to get us," someone said. We rapped out the SOS again. Ten of us are still alive in here. We've been here a day—a whole twenty-four hours in this awful place. We were thirty, but now we're ten. The others are gone.

We yelled to the men in the next compartment. The noise had been coming from that direction. Their excited replies told us they, too, thought rescue was on the way. Now the rapping started again, closer, stopped, started once more. We waited in an agony of suspense.

Abruptly, the silence of our compartment was broken as a yell sounded from the next compartment. Workers had broken through to them! They shouted to the rescue party that there were others trapped—us! We knocked frantically against the bulkhead! A voice was heard shouting above the clamor, "Can you stand a hole? We'll drill a small one through."

"Yes, yes, go ahead and drill!" A sailor flashed on the battle lantern. A hole appeared halfway up the bulkhead as the drill bit through the metal and then retreated. There was a loud hissing as the air pressure within and without equalized. The water began to pour in as the air rushed out! We had never thought of this. We could see the water flooding in through the hatch. Men jumped swiftly across the deck to close the hatch and dog it down. They secured it top and bottom, but water sprayed through the sides.

"Keep calm, fellows," a worker called. "We'll get you out!"

They began to cut through the metal. I watched, fascinated, tortured by the slow progress as the cut was made horizontal to the deck. We could see the blade push the cut along. Someone yelled, "Burn us out!" They replied, "No, you'd suffocate. Hold on! Hold on just a little longer!"

The water had risen to our knees. "Hurry! Hurry up!" we shouted as the downward cut began. I turned to look at the hatch. It was bulging inward at the center. Even that heavy metal could not withstand so great a water pressure. Would we all drown like rats at the last minute, just when rescue was at hand? It was going to be close, so close!

"Please hurry, for God's sake! We can't stop this flooding!" The cutting tool began its progress down the third side of the square. We watched, hypnotized. It was maddeningly slow. The water was now waist high. Would the hatch hold?

"We're going to bend it out," a voice spoke through the bulkhead. So close, yet a world away, separated from us by a quarter of an inch of steel, or less. It was the difference between life and death. Fingers pulled at the three-sided metal cut. I pushed at it. It was bending. There was no time to complete the cutting job. Gradually the opening widened as the water pushed at us from behind. It would be just wide enough to scrape through.

"Okay! Come on through!" voices called. We entered the opening in a flood of water. Friendly hands reached for our oil-slicked bodies and pulled us into the next compartment. We were free! Gratefully I searched the faces of our rescuers—big Hawaiian Navy Yard workers and some sailors. The Navy indeed took care of its own.

"Here, up on my shoulders, boy," said one of the men in the accent of the Islands. He smiled and I smiled back. "Thanks a lot," was all I could say. They boosted me from man to man and from space to space up through the bottom of the ship. Finally I emerged from out of the cold darkness into the warm sunshine of a new day. It was 0900, 8 December.

Standing on the upturned hull, I gazed about me. It was the same world I had left twenty-five hours before, but as I looked at the smoke and wreckage of battle, the sunken ships *Tennessee, West Virginia,* and *Arizona* astern of us, I felt that life would never be the same, not for me—not for any of us. I took a few drags on a cigarette. Someone said to put it out because of all the oil around.

A launch came alongside to take us to a hospital ship. As I stepped into the boat, I looked down at the ship we had lived in, the ship we had come so close to dying in, the tomb of friends and shipmates who were gone forever. The mighty *Oklahoma* was no more. The flag, the colored signal pennants would never fly again. Her guns were silent, her turrets full of men and water. How strange that never in all her life had she ever fired at an enemy.

The launch chugged along out into the harbor. Turning to the sailor who had bet a dollar with me on how we would die, I grinned at him. "Put the buck away for a souvenir, Willy. We both lost."

After Pearl Harbor, Seaman Young was assigned to the U.S.S. Honolulu *and served in the Guadalcanal and New Georgia campaigns. Later, commissioned in the Naval Reserve, he returned to action in the Korean War. Today he lives in Boston, writes military features for the Boston* Globe, *and is associated with a book publishing company. His memoir was originally published in* Proceedings, *the monthly magazine of the United States Naval Institute, and appears here by permission.*